Sharing the Bread of Life

Practical Help for All Who Speak in Public for God's Glory

Wentworth Pike

Gabriel
Publishing

Waynesboro, Georgia, U.S.A.

Recommendations for
Sharing the Bread of Life

We have been entrusted with a message of incalculable value. Since it's the most worthy message in the universe and we—inadequate though we be—are the message-bearers, we should eagerly learn to convey it more effectively. Wentworth Pike has written an interesting and highly practical guide to communicating God's truth. Sharing the Bread of Life *is simple, well-written, helpful, and Christ-honoring. I am glad to recommend it.*

Randy Alcorn
Eternal Perspective Ministries

An excellent book by my former professor and present team member, Rev. Wentworth Pike. This book will assist those wanting to learn to teach (and preach) God's Word clearly and effectively for the glory of God! It is an honor to recommend this helpful and very practical book by one who has served the Lord faithfully and with integrity as a Bible college professor, pastor, missionary, and writer.

Doug Nichols
International Director
ACTION International Ministries

© 2003 by Wentworth Pike

Published by Gabriel Publishing
PO Box 1047, 129 Mobilization Dr.
Waynesboro, GA 30830 U.S.A.
(706) 554-1594
gabriel@omlit.om.org

ISBN: 1-884543-76-6

Cover Design: Paul Lewis

Printed in the United States of America

Appreciation

Ray Woods, former Mayor of Williams Lake, British Columbia, and his wife, Karen, received the first draft of *Sharing the Bread of Life* about the time Ray discovered that cancer had returned. They had gladly agreed to proofread and offer constructive suggestions. I asked Karen to put the task aside, because it was too great a burden while they were staying in Vancouver during many weeks of Ray's incomplete surgery, radiation, and chemotherapy, but she replied that it was therapeutic for her as she spent long hours in waiting rooms. How can I possibly express my thanks to such dear friends? God bless you both, Ray and Karen.

Carol Tupper of Three Hills, Alberta, joyfully gave her talents by doing several sketches to illustrate *Sharing the Bread of Life*. I learned of Carol's abilities from her excellent illustrated gospel-tract booklets for youth. She is a graduate of Peace River Bible Institute in Sexsmith, Alberta. We look forward to seeing more of her work in literature and art for the Lord's glory. Thank you, Carol.

I am grateful also to Randy Alcorn, author and Founder/Director of Eternal Perspective Ministries, and to Doug Nichols, International Director of Action International Ministries (ACTION), for reviewing the book and offering helpful notations and personal recommendations.

Contents

Is This Book For You?

Possessing an "unquenchable desire to bring a passage of Scripture into contact with life,"[1] makes *Sharing the Bread of Life* a book for you.

Missionary Doreen Sears writes of the "intense need I feel to present the Word of God clearly and understandably." She says, "I want to present God's Word faithfully and truthfully...to give thinking, rational people the opportunity to understand God's love for the world in general and each of them in particular."[2] The purpose of *Sharing the Bread of Life* is to help you—business people and housewives, farmers and professionals, believers in all walks of life—who share that "intense need" to wield the Sword of the Spirit effectively against Satan.

Arthur Mathews, missionary statesman and author, said, "There is nothing that Jesus used to defeat Satan that is not available to us."[3] In Matthew 4:4, Jesus says, "It is written: 'Man does not live on bread alone, but on every word that comes from the mouth of God.'"

Sharing the Bread of Life includes the following:

- Reading Scripture aloud effectively.
- Giving devotional talks.
- Outlining Scripture passages for effective teaching.
- Finding apt illustrations.

- Leading discussion groups.
- Preaching.
- And more, much more!

Harold Peters, Vice President of Field Ministries for Gospel Missionary Union, writes, "…a major impediment to the advance of the gospel in Western Europe is the fact that many Europeans think that it is the role of a paid professional to spread the Word. In North America, churches count on much of their ministry being done by lay people who work alongside pastors and other church leaders to witness, teach, and preach the Word of God."[4]

William M. Easum, Senior Consultant for 21st Century Strategies, Inc.writes regarding what we may expect concerning the Church in the twenty-first century. He says the following:

> The 21st Century Church will be led mostly by pastors who received their training on the field rather than in the seminary classroom…. My estimate is that two-thirds of the pastors of the largest churches in North America have never been to seminary. Around the globe, the percentage would be even higher. Non-Christians seem to respond best to leaders who can communicate with them on their level more than leaders with academic credentials.[5]

On June 9, 2001, the *New York Times* carried an article called "Demand Is Rising for Clergy as Fewer Answer the Calling," by Gustav Neibuhr. "Until recently," Neibuhr observed, "…a number of churches…are finding that filling vacancies takes much longer than it once did, and the pool of candidates has shrunk. Some never find the leaders they seek."

The *New York Times* writer adds, "…many of [the] evangelical churches have lately undertaken efforts to train lay people to serve as pastors…."

This is one important reason why *Sharing the Bread of Life* is needed—and needed *now*.

Sharing the Bread of Life will benefit the following groups and individuals:

1. Sunday school teachers, youth leaders, and home Bible-study leaders.
2. Pastors, evangelists, lay pastors, chaplains, mentors, disciple makers, career missionaries, and short-term missionaries.
3. Elders, deacons, campus leaders and students.
4. Rescue mission speakers, open-air preachers.
5. Those who speak in jails, hospitals, and seniors' homes.
6. All who share God's Word with large or small groups.
7. Anyone who wants to speak well for Christ before a group.

Dale Carnegie taught hundreds of thousands of people to overcome self-consciousness, fright, confusion, inability to concentrate, and memory failure. They gained self-confidence, poise, and the ability to think on their feet. They acquired the ability to arrange their thoughts in logical order and to speak clearly and convincingly before business and social groups. His book, *The Quick and Easy Way to Effective Speaking,*[6] continues to be on best-seller lists because it is simple, easy to read, and easy to put into practice. However, the believer who speaks for Christ has far greater resources than anyone who speaks on secular topics.

Some declare the number one phobia in the world is not the fear of fire or of drowning, but the fear of standing up before a group of people and speaking. Yet ordinary people on talk shows reaching millions have no trouble talking before a studio audience, TV cameras, and microphones. Why? Two reasons: (1) They have something to say that is important to them. (2) They are excited about what they are saying.

Is the Bible important to you? Are you excited about God's Word? If the answer is yes, claim God's promise in Matthew 7:7, 8, "Ask and it will be given to you; seek and you will find; knock and the door will be opened to you. For everyone who asks receives; he who seeks finds; and to him who knocks, the door will be opened." Soon your problem with self-confidence will take a back seat to Christ-consciousness: "I can do everything through him who gives me strength" (Philippians 4:13). Your confidence is in Him. Pray, study God's Word, arrange your thoughts, and know beyond any doubt that the Holy Spirit within you is in control! Jesus promised that the Holy Spirit, "will guide you into all truth.... He will bring glory to me by taking from what is mine and making it known to you" (John 16:13-14).

When you use a Sunday school quarterly or other commentary on the Scriptures, never let it replace the Bible itself. Encourage your class to study directly from their Bibles with their quarterlies. Use the teacher's quarterly only for a study help with your Bible open; then teach from your open Bible.

You may always have some tension before you speak. That's good! A snail does not seem to be very tense. A thoroughbred horse is!

Once when I turned on the TV, I saw men trying to get the last horse into the starting gate for The Breeders' Championship Race at Churchill Downs. All the other horses were in their places, but the European champion—the horse that the owner hoped would soon be world champion—was so feisty that eight to ten men were frantically trying to get him into starting position. No, champions aren't docile! But tension must be controlled in order to win the race. Controlled tension is dynamic. Dale Carnegie said that a person who claims always "to be as cool as a cucumber" before speaking is probably "about as inspiring as a cucumber."[7] You have the Bread of Life to share. It is...

- a lifeline for a drowning person,
- a glass of cold water for one dying of thirst,
- a word of wisdom for one who lacks it,
- counsel for youth,

- hope for the discouraged, depressed, and desperate,
- the inspired Word of the living God for all mankind.

You have direct access to the indwelling Holy Spirit for dynamic direction and divine power. Wherever you speak, may God bless your preparation and witness with the Holy Spirit's anointing.

No, the favored horse did not win! He came in third. And you won't win them all either. Sometimes you will wonder whether it is worth all the effort, but there will be a crown for you to lay at Jesus' feet. As Dr. Helen Roseveare, veteran missionary with WEC Int., corrects us, "Don't ask, 'Is it worth it?' Ask, 'Is He worthy?'"

Obey and claim 2 Timothy 2:15, "Do your best to present yourself to God as one approved, a workman who does not need to be ashamed and who correctly handles the word of truth." Pray that God will give you wisdom (James 1:5) to glorify Him as you speak (John 14:13; 17:1).

In the fellowship of Calvary's bonds,
Wentworth Pike

CHAPTER **1**

Speak for Christ

To share the Bread of Life effectively, we need wisdom. Someone has said that the secret of effective prayer is prayer in secret. It is surely the secret for obtaining wisdom: "If any of you lacks wisdom, he should ask of God, who gives generously to all without finding fault, and it will be given to him" (James 1:5). What a simple method! What a profound promise!

"Now go; I will help you speak and I will teach you what to say" (Exodus 4:12).

Your Personal Testimony

Skills are the result of teaching and doing. Do not try to fly an airplane without taking lessons; do not apply to an airline for a flying job without experience. We learn to walk by walking, to swim by swimming, to speak by speaking. Practice. There is no other way. Give a testimony in church, Sunday school class, home Bible study, or in private. But get started.

Invite a couple or a family, saved or unsaved, to Sunday dinner. Quote something the pastor said in the morning sermon, whether or not they were present. During the conversation, tell them what Jesus means to you.

Oh, yes you can! If you can talk about Saturday's ball game or your favorite recipe, you can talk about Sunday's sermon. If you can talk about camping last summer, you can talk about what happened to you when Christ came into your life. Satan does not want you to do it, so it is more difficult at first. Pray for Holy Spirit wisdom and courage. Follow Jesus' example in Matthew 4:1-11. (Go ahead; look it up and read it. You will need to open your Bible often while reading *Sharing the Bread of Life*.)

For a clear-cut testimony, plan it but do not memorize it. If you are a beginner, read a verse of Scripture. Then talk about what the Lord has done for you. A sentence or two about your salvation or a recent blessing is enough. You may read a verse from a hymn to summarize what the Lord means to you. The following sample is a good, Christ-centered testimony:

> Romans 10:13 says, "Everyone who calls on the name of the Lord will be saved." I thank the Lord for saving me. "Amazing grace! How sweet the sound. that saved a wretch like me! I once was lost, but now am found, was blind but now I see."[8]

A Scripture verse, a sentence to make it personal, a verse of a song will make a powerful testimony. Or stop with the verse and a personal sentence.

In a personal conversation, find an opening for your testimony by listening to the other person. Ask about his life, his home area, hobbies, travels, or business interests.

In a New York City airport, I prayed silently, "Lord, give me someone to listen to as I fly to Holland." Then I thought, "Why did I say that? I should have asked for someone to witness to." As I started to re-phrase my request, there was a check in my spirit. "No," I decided, "I will leave it that way, 'someone to listen to.'"

The Jewish man next to me on the 747 was a buyer of precious gems for a large company. He was also a talker. I thought, "Lord, you surely answered that prayer!" For about two and a half hours, he told me about the book he had written on his philosophy of life. He was not an orthodox Jew. His prolonged "philosophy" was merely salvation by works—the same as any unsaved Gentile. All

I had opportunity to say was an occasional comment: "Is that right?" "Oh?" "I see." "Well, that is interesting."

"Would you be interested in hearing my philosophy of life?" I finally asked when he paused.

"What? Your philosophy of life?" (What could he say after I had shown polite interest in his long monologue?) "Oh, yes, sure."

"What if it is opposed to your philosophy?"

"What do you mean?" he asked.

"It is not mine in the sense of having created it. Someone gave it to me and I accepted it. That is what makes it mine. Will you be offended if it contradicts yours?" I probed.

"Oh, no—no, of course not." He was obviously perplexed as to how any thinking person could have a life philosophy that contradicted his own. "Please explain your philosophy to me."

Wow! Had the Holy Spirit set him up or what?

I opened my New Testament to Ephesians 2:8, 9, 10. Too often we stop short of verse 10. I wanted him to see that the only good works that God will accept are those *produced by faith in Jesus Christ.* Salvation cannot be earned. It must be received by grace through faith. Good works follow.

My Jewish seatmate did not receive Christ as his Messiah-Savior that night. He obviously had never before heard the gospel clearly presented and his heart was not yet prepared for a decision. However, he gladly accepted the gift of my leather-bound New Testament with the promise to read it.

Ask the Lord for wisdom and an open door to share your personal testimony whether with one person or more. He will, and you will be sharing the Bread of Life effectively.

The Aim

The archer must have a target. The football player must know where his goal line is. And the teacher must have an aim.

Without a target the archer's arrows may fly in any direction, accomplish nothing, damage something, or harm someone. When an athlete became confused about where his goal line was, he ran many yards only to score for his opponent. The Apostle Paul said, "Similarly, if anyone competes as an athlete, he does not receive the victor's crown unless he competes according to the rules" (2 Timothy 2:5). Without an aim for each lesson a schoolteacher will discover that students' standard achievement test scores at the end of the term have not advanced very much since the beginning of the term, and some will have regressed. A Christian speaker must be no less diligent in knowing and striving for the goal than the archer, the football player, or the schoolteacher.

Along the mountainous border of Alberta and British Columbia in Canada, a stream on the Continental Divide is so tiny that one can step across it in places. It divides into two brooks which join "the Pacific and Arctic drainage on the west" and "the Arctic and Atlantic drainage on the east."[9] Many unimpressive streams feed a mighty river. The river can carry a nation's commerce only because each stream contributes its flow.

So each part of a speech should contribute some idea to the speaker's aim. Whether it is a speech to inform, to entertain, or to persuade, each outline division, explanation, and illustration should help the speaker along toward his goal. A discussion leader, Sunday school teacher, or preacher must have a conviction about what the Lord wants to accomplish through the discussion or talk and design every part with that goal in view.

Jesus had one ultimate goal. He said, "Here I am—it is written about me in the scroll—I have come to do your will, O God" (Hebrews 10:7). "And I will do whatever you ask in my name, so that the Son may bring glory to the Father" (John 14:13). "Father, the time has come. Glorify your Son, that your Son may glorify you" (John 17:1). In life or in death, in His teaching or His miracles, in joy or in sorrow—in all that He thought, spoke, or did—Jesus had one goal: the Father's glory. "So whether you eat or drink or whatever you do, do it all for the glory of God" (1 Corinthians 10:31).

In speaking for Christ our supreme goal must always be that God might receive the glory. "To glorify God and to enjoy Him forever," is the way our forefathers said it. How He is to be glorified should be expressed in our specific aim as we prepare to share the Bread of Life.

The Knowledge Aim

Knowledge of God's Word is an aim the Lord Himself established throughout the Bible.

To the Israelites He commanded, "These commandments that I give you today are to be upon your hearts. Impress them on your children. Talk about them when you sit at home and when you walk along the road, when you lie down and when you get up" (Deuteronomy 6:6-7).

In Psalm 119, verse eleven summarizes all 176 verses, "I have hidden your word in my heart that I might not sin against you." The Books of Wisdom acknowledge that wise actions can proceed only from knowledge of God's words, "For the Lord gives wisdom, and from his mouth come knowledge and understanding" (Proverbs 2:6).

Jesus continually stressed the importance of Scripture knowledge. In the wilderness He repeatedly fired strategic shots against that archenemy, Satan, by declaring, "It is written…" His first such quotation from the Old Testament should be the foundation of sharing the Bread of Life: "It is written, 'Man does not live on bread alone, but on every word that comes from the mouth of God'" (Matthew 4:4; Deuteronomy 8:3).

Paul, the learned, refused to rely on his own worldly philosophical and theological education, but placed highest value on the knowledge of God and His will (1 Corinthians 1:18-2:16). He wrote to the Colossian believers, "We have not stopped praying for you and asking God to fill you with the knowledge of his will through all spiritual wisdom and understanding" (Colossians 2:9).

Write your Knowledge Aim so it will be sharp in your own mind as you prepare and as you speak. Word it something like this: "*I want my hearers to know* that God invites all sinners to be saved by His grace." Do not clutter your aim with too many words. Hit the bull's-eye. What do you want people to *know*? Following are sample Knowledge Aims:

- "I want my students to know John 3:16 word-perfect."
- "I want my class to know that heaven and hell are real places."
- "I want the congregation to know that the Holy Spirit is a Person, not an impersonal force or influence."
- "I want each individual to know in his or her heart the assurance of personal salvation."
- "I want my audience to know that God is three Persons in one Godhead."
- "I want my youth group to know that God is working in all things for the good of those who love Him, who have been called according to His purpose."
- "I want my preschoolers to know that God loves them."

Of course, there are many levels of knowledge. We know facts. We know methods and procedures. We know people, some as acquaintances, some as friends, and still others on a deeper level as family members. We discern truth from falsehood. "Now, I know in part; then shall I know fully, even as I am fully known" (1 Corinthians 13:12). Let's make it our aim to increase knowledge.

The Inspiration Aim
We should never be satisfied when our congregation or our students acquire head knowledge. People have emotions, even as they have knowledge and volition (will) because people are made in God's image. He is a personal God. He has knowledge, emotions, and volition. Therefore, we do also. Proper appeal to the emotions is scriptural. The Inspiration Aim expresses the way I want my hearers to feel.

A worthy aim is, "I want my hearers to respond to God's holiness in deep awe and humility."

Here are a few examples of the Inspiration Aim:

- "I want them to love the Lord with all their heart, soul, mind, and strength."
- "I want them to 'love one another deeply, from the heart.'"
- "I want them to develop joyful perseverance (stick-to-it determination) in faith."
- "I want them to have deep compassion for the poor, the sick, the grieving and the lost."
- "I want them habitually to cast all their fears, worries and anxieties on the Lord."
- "I want them to 'rejoice with those who rejoice and mourn with those who mourn.'"
- "I want them to glory in Christ and put no faith in the flesh."
- "I want them to 'rejoice in the Lord always.'"

The Conduct-Response Aim

Jesus, the Master Teacher, did not stop with imparting knowledge and inspiring good feelings. He often discomfited the comfortable and upset the ritualistic religious rulers who prided themselves in their knowledge of the law. He warned of the pharisaic leaven of hypocrisy and described Pharisees as whitewashed tombs full of dead men's bones (cf. Matthew 23:27).

Jesus' purpose in sharing the Bread of Life was to motivate change in behavior. Yes, knowledge of our sinful condition is necessary. Yes, sorrow has its place. But without repentance, of what value are knowledge and emotion? Our ultimate goal must be changed lives. Some prefer to call this the Behavioral Aim.

A sampling of possible Conduct-Response Aims follows:

- "I want sinners to turn to Christ for salvation."
- "I want my hearers to develop an effective prayer ministry."
- "I want believers to give generously."

- "I want my group to become soul-winners."
- "I want them to become personally involved in missions."
- "I want some to volunteer for career missionary service."
- "I want each member to have daily Bible-reading and prayer."
- "I want fathers to take responsibility for spiritual leadership."
- "I want families to establish daily family devotions."
- "I want these young people to make a heart commitment to God to keep themselves sexually pure from this day on."
- "I want Christians to forgive as they want to be forgiven."

There are short-term aims and long-range goals. For example, you may have a Knowledge Aim for the next three meetings, an Inspiration Aim for the fourth meeting, and a Conduct-Response Aim for the fifth time you get together. Or the Holy Spirit may lead you to begin with an Inspiration Aim that will issue in a desire for more knowledge. For a single lesson, you may have as your aim that sinners will come to Christ for salvation (Conduct-Response), but you will endeavor to establish knowledge of biblical truth and seek the Holy Spirit's conviction for sin before you can make that evangelistic appeal. In such case, Conduct-Response is your aim and acquiring knowledge becomes your method.

Each lesson should have a definite aim—knowledge, inspiration or conduct-response—one you can write in a simple clause or sentence. What do you want as a result of your talk? What do you want people to know? To feel? To do? That is your target. Zero in on that. *Write it in a simple sentence.* Then, prayerfully decide ways to determine achievement of individual lesson aims that show progress toward long-range goals.

Each series of lessons, studies or sermons should have a specific Behavioral or Conduct-Response aim. Establish your aims in prayer and Bible study. Know your aims. Keep your immediate aim foremost in your preparation and speaking or leading a discussion. Never lose sight of your ultimate aim or goal: The Glory of God! But that is not enough. You need to be specific. *How* do you plan for His glory?

Teachers, even secular teachers, need aims related to the students' needs, interests and abilities. Do *not* choose "Understanding the major doctrines of the Bible" as your Knowledge Aim for preschoolers. Have practical aims that you can measure or test to see whether you are reaching them. Such measurements and tests will probably come through out-of-class interaction of teacher and student. Make the sacrifice of time, effort, and expense for extracurricular activities. However, pray for the power of the Holy Spirit to achieve spiritual goals in each student's life that go far beyond anything you can measure or test during the time you interact with the student.

If you are as blessed in ways this author has been, you will see results beyond the limits of your imagination. But many will come years later. What joy it is to be a prayer partner with seasoned missionaries, men and women of God, who were my average high-school students thirty years ago! May God also grant you such joy.

CHAPTER 2

Share God's Word

The Holy Spirit's use of Scripture convicts, comforts and encourages. Nothing in the lesson, sermon, Bible study, or devotional talk is more important than reading directly from the Bible to convey what God says. Few Christian speakers read Scripture well in front of an audience. What *we* say *about* the Bible has value only as we proclaim and clarify "every word that comes from the mouth of God" (Matthew 4:4).

From the moment we start, even before we read or say anything, we communicate with our bodies as well as our voices. Posture, facial expression, enunciation (articulation), and voice communicate positive or negative messages.

Sit Tall; Stand Tall.

When reading the Bible to a small group such as a home Bible study, sit where all can see and hear. If you cannot see everyone's face in a room, stand where you can see each one and all can see you.

Stand erect. Relax, but do not slouch to one side or lean on a pulpit. *Erect* does not mean *rigid.* Whether sitting or standing, correct posture is vital for at least four reasons:

1. Good posture indicates the authority of God's Word. (Poor posture appears apologetic; it has a negative impact.)

2. Posture affects how clearly you speak.
3. Good posture makes your voice resonant and pleasing.
4. Good posture makes it possible to project your voice so that it carries clearly to everyone.

UNST(E)ADY

LE(A)NING

A K(I)(M)BO

RELAXED, ERECT

Communicate with the Members of Your Body.

It is important to remember that you are communicating a message to your group before you begin to speak, as you are speaking, and as you return to your seat. You are conveying by your body an impression, either positive or negative, when you are sitting, standing, or walking. How you walk and stand, whether you have eye contact with your audience as you speak, and what you are doing with your hands are all important all of the time.

Your feet. Place your feet comfortably apart. Feet too close together create an unsteady appearance and an insecure feeling. Standing with feet wide apart and arms akimbo in a macho stance is fine for a cowboy on the range, but it attracts undo attention to a speaker's platform posture and detracts from what he says.

Your eyes. Pause and look at your audience. Wait a moment before you speak. Silence will get attention. Shouting will not! It may get the appearance of attention, but it will increase mental disturbance and lower your group's respect for you! You will lose even any superficial attention gained when you lower your voice again.

Establish eye contact. We communicate with our eyes. Smile. Your audience will know that you like them. Do not talk until you have everyone's attention. They will know that you are in control and speak with authority. *Keep that eye contact.* Yes, even while reading Scripture! If you hold your Bible chest-high, away from your body, you can read more distinctly. You will not muffle words by reading into the open Bible. Nor will you cut off resonance by bending your chin down. (Resonance is the quality that makes your voice carry well to everyone and makes it pleasant to hear.) You can frequently look above the Bible at your audience.

Look first at one person and then another, to one part of the room, then another—not a fleeting glance and not staring. Avoid a pattern. Vary your eye contact. If you spoke directly to Mr. Smith the last time, look at Mrs. Jones the next time around.

Warm, personal eye contact makes everyone feel that you are speaking directly to him or her, even when the crowd is large and eye contact can be established with only some individuals. We feel uncomfortable carrying on a conversation with a person who constantly avoids eye contact with us. An audience quickly loses interest if you look out the window, at the ceiling, at a spot on the back wall, down at the floor, or at a desktop.

With your Bible chest-high, you will not have to look down at a pulpit or table. Hold it low enough so you can speak above it but can lower your eyes to the page without ducking your head. Looking down at your Bible on a pulpit or a table will muffle your voice. You will not be able to project it to the farthest corners of the room. Instead, you will speak into the pages of a book, shorten your breath, and limit the number of people who can hear all of your words. Learn to project (push) your voice without shouting. There are usually some people who are hard of hearing.

Your hands. Keep your hands out of your pockets! When a speaker has the habit of putting first one hand and then the other into a pocket, that is what we remember. If your hands make you nervous and you do not know what to do with them, place your fingertips gently on the stand or table in front of you, but *do not lean on it.* (This repetition is deliberate!)

Once you put your Bible down use both hands freely to gesture for emphasis or to describe something. Keep the gestures higher than your waist and higher than a stand in front of you. A strong gesture does far more for emphasis than either shouting or lowering your voice. Weak, low gestures detract from what you are saying instead of emphasizing it. Watch preschoolers as they talk. They use effective gestures naturally. Only learned self-consciousness causes us not to gesture freely.

Use your imagination for the following *pretend* actions and practice them in private or with a friend to relearn the effective use of gestures:

1. Throw a make-believe baseball to a person a long distance away.
2. Throw a large ball to a preschooler five feet from you.
3. Pick up a 100 pound sack of cement, carry it across the room and stack it on the floor.
4. Bounce a ball on the floor.
5. Act out an "I don't know" attitude with both hands outstretched with palms up and a shrug of the shoulders.
6. Show a negative attitude, such as refusal, non-approval or dislike by palms down or thumbs down.
7. Greet a friend whom you have not seen for several years and were not expecting to see.
8. Wave goodbye.
9. Try on a new coat in front of a mirror.

10. Salute the flag proudly as it passes in a parade.

Although you can use only one hand to gesture while holding the Bible, you will need both hands when you put it down. Usually, it is best to have both hands free.

Study each of the four sketches that follow. Why has the universal "Wrong Way" sign been added to the first three? Explain why each would detract from reading Scripture to an audience.

Announce the Reference Well.

Give people time to find the place in their Bibles. Otherwise, we defeat our purpose in four ways:

1. If people are still looking for the passage while we are reading, they miss the whole meaning.
2. People will not connect our explanation later with the text and will not grasp our meaning.

3. People feel frustrated locating the place while the speaker is already reading. Frustration makes minds unreceptive.
4. Some give up. Closing their Bibles, they do not follow as we expound the Scriptures.

There are simple ways to avoid such problems:

* Announce the reference slowly and clearly as follows:

"First Corinthians chapter one,
verses eighteen through twenty-five."

* Pause while people start looking in their Bibles. Then repeat the reference in different words as follows:

"That is the Apostle Paul's first letter to the
Corinthians, chapter one. We will begin
reading at verse eighteen."

* While slower ones are locating the place, the speaker can give two or three sentences of background information that will not interfere with their search. Finally, the speaker should give the reference the third time briefly before starting to read:

"First Corinthians one, eighteen."

Following this simple procedure is not a waste of time. Not following it wastes both time and attention. To begin reading when the congregation is still looking for the passage is to squander God's Word rather than to declare it clearly and effectively.

In a Bible study where unsaved friends are present use Bibles that are alike and announce the page number of the text.

TIP:
**If you want people to look up a verse,
mention the reference *first* and allow time to find it.
If you do not want to wait for them to find it,
do not mention the reference until
after you have read or quoted the verse,
and they will not look it up.
*Try it. It works!***

Be Enthusiastic About God's Word.

Another of Carnegie's principles was, "Be sure you are excited about your subject."[10] In his day the average person thought of public speaking as "elocution" by silver-tongued orators who spent years learning proper breathing techniques and vocal intonation. Carnegie, seeing the futility of that for busy people in the workaday world, approached public speaking as a skill any person of normal intelligence could develop. That produced results.

If politicians and salesmen can be enthusiastic about their wares because they are excited about them, shouldn't Christian workers do as well—or better?

People will listen if *you* believe what you are saying with all your heart. You can't fake it. Lasting enthusiasm for sharing will not come from a mountaintop experience. As we digest the Bread of Life daily and assimilate it into our own lives, claim its promises in prayer, and see them fulfilled, we will be eager to share it with the hungry.

CHAPTER **3**

Share Effectively

Whether you speak to entertain, inform, or persuade, you need to know some things about your audience. The better you know them and their needs, the more effectively you can speak to them.

The Speech to Entertain

A speech to entertain? By a *Christian* speaker? Why not?

One Bible college teacher had no use for any speech training in the curriculum except homiletics—the art of preaching. He didn't think the speech to entertain, the speech to inform, and the speech to persuade had any place in a Bible college.

With all due respect, I wholeheartedly disagree!

When I was in high school, I memorized a three-minute hilarious monologue on golf, complete with dialect and extravagant actions. For over half a century, at just-for-fun get-togethers it has met with guffaws from all ages.

What does that have to do with sharing the Bread of Life? It has opened many doors for me to share. On the first day at children's Bible camp, when some were scared and some were homesick, my monologue changed tears and scowls to excited laughter and the expectation of fun to come. Later, when I spoke to them from God's Word, they listened.

Then, there is the one I call My Four Bears—not a speech

about my ancestors—four short stories about real experiences with bears. Even the locations create interest—Alaska, the Canadian Rocky Mountains, Yellowstone National Park in Wyoming, and Lincoln National Forest in New Mexico. You can use your own entertaining experiences.

A reading such as "Casey at the Bat," "Who's On First?" or Robert Service's poem, "The Cremation of Sam McGee," is worth memorizing so you can use it on a moment's notice. A poem, a story, a humorous reading. They break down reserve with adults as well as attracting children's interest. Check out the possibilities in your local library. They are wholesome fun. And they are bait on the hook!

The Speech to Inform

Whatever your hobby or area of expertise is, there are those who would be delighted to hear you speak about it—at community events, neighborhood fellowship dinners, boys' clubs, girls' clubs, or seniors' homes. Then when you have opportunity to share the Bread of Life with them, you won't be a stranger. Do you crochet, knit, or decorate cakes? How about welding? Have you traveled somewhere? Giving cooking lessons or just sharing favorite recipes can open many doors. Christians need to be seen, not as people who have a lot of "don'ts" and go to church, but as community members who share interests with others. Giving a speech to inform—even if only a brief one—may open doors to unregenerate hearts that you would never contact through your Sunday school class.

The purpose of the speech to inform is merely to share information. Stick to one subject. Open with something humorous, a startling statement, a believe-it-or-not fact, a human-interest story, or a sincere word of appreciation for being invited to share what you have learned about the subject. Know your audience. Consider age, gender, and special interests.

In a county in Georgia I have a standing invitation to speak at a monthly luncheon at a government-funded, countywide senior citizen's center. Because of the separation of church and state, the matron is not free to invite me to preach. But when I interviewed her about functions of the center that might benefit my aged mother, I mentioned some of the places I had traveled. She asked whether I could speak to the large group of seniors who gather for the noon meal and games.

"How would a travelogue do?" I asked.

"Oh, that would be wonderful."

"And I can tell them about the street children our mission works with in Third-World countries."

"Oh, yes, please do. They will like that!"

There are now believers from that group who pray faithfully for our ministry, and all are delighted to welcome us when we return. Meet them where they are, and share Christ with them when you can. No compromise with sin and worldliness need be involved.

The Speech to Persuade

Mothers are the best! Listen when they tell their children to stay out of the mud, pick up their clothes, or do their homework. Encyclopedia salesmen aren't bad examples either. They are a little more subtle, but certainly persuasive. I know; I used to be one. I never sold anyone an encyclopedia unless they wanted it, but after my demonstration, they wanted it!

Why do some preachers, Sunday school teachers, and Bible study leaders speak to inform but never to persuade? One almost feels that they think, as unsaved people often do, that we should not try to persuade anyone. One would think that there must be a verse somewhere that says, "Thou shalt give information only and let people decide for themselves. Thou shalt not seek to persuade anyone." But you will have to go to Hezekiah 1:1 or take Human Philosophy 101 to find it, because it is not in the Bible!

"Since, then, we know what it is to fear the Lord, we try to persuade men" (2 Corinthians 5:11). Away with nonsense about not persuading children—or grownups either!

A speech to persuade should be solidly based on a reasonable presentation of facts. To persuade sinners to be saved and saints to live godly lives the speech must be rooted in a logical presentation of Scripture. Above all, it must be bathed with prayer for the persuasion of the Holy Spirit. Jesus said of the Holy Spirit, "When he comes, he will convict [convince, persuade] the world of guilt in regard to sin and righteousness and judgment" (John 16:8).

Guiding the Learner

"Teaching is not telling," so educators *tell* us! Do you see something contradictory in that statement? But there is a lot of truth in it. Let's examine it.

My cousin Charles was about four years old when he used to shoo all the chickens into one corner of the fenced-in chicken yard. Then he stood on a stump and preached to them. Who can say he was not preaching? But was he teaching?

One day Charles' grandmother left him in the car while she went into a store to buy a spool of thread. She knew she would be gone a very short time, so she didn't think he would have time to get into trouble. What should she find upon her return, after making her way through the crowd but Charles standing beside the car holding a street meeting! He preached more gospel with the verses he had memorized than some men of the cloth preach from their pulpits. He had preached; he had entertained; but had he taught?

We cannot say that we have taught unless someone has learned. There is no teaching unless learning is taking place. When we merely *tell,* we usually have no way of knowing whether anyone has learned. We cannot say that someone has learned until behavior has changed. Change in behavior may be slight or great; it may be conversion (an about face), change of direction, or it may be growth.

Then, too, there are various kinds, or levels, of learning. A test to determine whether those to whom we have talked have actually learned might only determine whether they have learned

to parrot back the answers we programmed them to repeat—
rote learning. There is no proof that such learning becomes part of
one's behavior.

Think. Suppose a child is accustomed to saying, "I ain't got
no marbles to play with." His schoolteacher instructs him that he
should say, "I do not have any marbles." On the playground, when
his buddies challenge him to a game, what will he reply? Having
been a schoolteacher for some years, I have no doubt that his
reply would run something like this: "I ain't got all my marbles."
(And if some people think otherwise, they have probably lost a
few!) Desirable learning has not happened until behavior has
changed for the better.

A child has learned that he should not run into the street to get
his ball without looking both ways or he might be killed. That is a
fact he has learned. But suppose that one day a car kills his puppy.
Now, his learning has reached a much deeper level. No longer a
cold fact, the learning has become internalized knowledge and
understanding.

Ivan Petrovich Pavlov (1849-1936), Nobel prize-winner in
physiology and life-long student of brain functions, demonstrated
learning on a level he called a *conditioned reflex*. If a bell rang
and food was introduced in that order repeatedly, a dog would
soon salivate when the bell rang. By association, the dog had
learned that a bell ringing meant food was coming.

An infant may cry instinctively when she is wet, in pain or
hungry. But she soon learns from association that milk is delivered
when she cries, and crying for food becomes a conditioned reflex.

There are levels of learning such as factual learning, conditioning
by association, rote learning, experiential learning through trial and
error, and reasoning from a premise to a conclusion. Hearing helps
learning but observing often helps more.

When my wife and I taught all the grades in a small Eskimo
village school, we learned. We learned that Eskimos (at least in
our area) did not teach their children by answering questions.
Questions were not part of their culture. We also learned that they

did not teach their children by telling so much as by giving opportunities to observe. When they wanted children to learn something, they showed them or assumed they would learn by watching their parents and older siblings.

Some anthropologists have written about this as though Eskimo parents never *tell* their children, but rely solely on observation and experience. Well, I can't say how much Eskimo parents had picked up from white men, but I have certainly seen an Eskimo father lecture his small infant. When the public health nurse flew into the village to give inoculations, all the mothers brought their children to the school for "shots." A mother held her baby across her knees while the nurse gave the injection at one end and the father lectured to the other.

What did he say? He taught a basic essential of arctic survival: "Eskimo don't cry! Eskimo don't cry! You don't cry!" If, as former generations believed, there is truth in the old adage, "Repetition is the mother of learning," that baby must have learned well. I am not sure how he sorted out the contradictory learning he was receiving—experience at one end and repetition at the other! But the fact is I have never seen an Eskimo cry, other than infants, except when the Holy Spirit produced repentance unto salvation. The following are three examples:

Although Daniel Seetook was sixteen years old, he was in the eighth grade. His schooling had been delayed while he spent time in a tuberculosis hospital far from home. Daniel wanted to be a missionary to his own people, but when I asked him whether he had received the Lord Jesus Christ as his own Savior, tears began trickling down his face. He repented of his sins and believed the gospel for himself that afternoon. That was the first time I had seen an Eskimo non-infant cry.

The next time was when his adoptive father, Seetook, stood before the congregation in the rough-hewn little church on the beach of the Bering Strait and related how Daniel, the boy the family had made their slave, had led him and his wife to Christ. The tears flowed down his cheeks as he spoke. When the Holy

Spirit works deeply in the hearts of people, it is not unusual for the wells of the great deep to be broken up—even for a stoic Eskimo.

After a young man, Carl, was saved, he borrowed my tape recorder to record his testimony for his former drinking buddies in Nome. On it he said, "You got to cry when you get saved." Of course, he had no Scripture for that, but it probably had its roots in his learning from infancy, "Eskimo don't cry!"

Learning takes place on many levels and by many means in daily life. God has given you the commission to "Go and preach the gospel to all creation" (Mark 16:15). However, another time He worded the Great Commission thus: "Therefore go and make disciples of all nations...teaching them..." (Matthew 28:19, 20).

We must not reduce our idea of teaching simply to *telling*. If learning involves hearing, observing, and most of all experiencing, then teaching must *guide* the learner. Throughout the Old Testament and the New Testament the Lord is depicted as the One who guides. Psalm 23:2-3 says, "He leads me beside quiet waters.... He guides me in paths of righteousness for His name's sake." Psalm 48:14, "For this God is our God for ever and ever; He will be our guide even to the end." And in John 10 we read Jesus' description of Himself as the Good Shepherd who "calls His own sheep by name and leads them out."

The teacher's goal, then, must always be to guide. Guide your students by your life, and guide them in the Word of God. Then you will be sharing the Bread of Life effectively.

Preaching and teaching are interwoven ministries. The Apostle Paul said of Jesus our Lord, "It was he who gave...some to be pastors and teachers" (Ephesians 4:11). Many Bible scholars understand this to refer to believers whom the Lord intended to fill both roles—pastor and teacher. Blessed be the congregations who have pastor/teachers.

Sharing the Bread of Life is the activity to which believers are called. Share the Bread with individual children, youth, and adults, with couples, families, and groups small and large at every opportunity.

CHAPTER **4**

Vary Your Methods

Preaching is a form of lecture. Paul said that Christ sent him to preach and that "God was pleased through the foolishness of what was preached to save those who believed" (1 Corinthians 1:21). There is no substitute for God's ordained method of preaching.

Jesus, the Master Teacher, preached. He also taught by the question-and-answer method and by discussion. He enhanced His teaching by object lessons (a coin, fish, farming, the wind—a sort of show-and-tell method using common things people knew) and illustrated profusely with parables.

What is the best method of teaching—lecture, question-and-answer, discussion, or the use of visual aids and story illustrations? Turn the question around. What is the worst method? Answer: The method that is used every week with no variety. Too often in Sunday school this is the lecture method with no discussion, few illustrations, no object lessons and no questions. In other words, the weakest method of teaching is whatever method fails to make learning easier and more exciting. It is also one that gives no opportunity for feedback to determine what the group is learning.

Some teachers do all the talking. Just before the dismissal bell they say, "If any of you have anything to say, just speak up." But no one returns from a mental golf game or daydreaming about the roast beef dinner with anything to say.

Other teachers of adult or teen Sunday school classes would like lively discussion, so they try to stimulate it by thought-provoking questions. However, if the group is accustomed to weekly lectures, they will not readily be converted to discussion without patient preparation over a period of weeks.

A man called me long-distance concerning my book, *Principles of Effective Prayer*. His son, a missionary, had sent it as a gift with the suggestion that he might want to use it in his adult Sunday school class. When he asked me what I thought would be the best way to teach it, I called his attention to the section entitled *Study and Discussion Questions* at the end of each lesson. I advised him to have the group read the lesson and prepare for the discussion questions before class. If possible, small groups of seven or eight persons are most effective. I said that each couple or single person would need a copy of the book.

However, the class did not order more books. Instead, without further class preparation, the teacher launched the class of over 100 members into discussion by using the *Study and Discussion Questions* that followed chapter one, although they had not read the lesson. Obviously, they liked their teacher. But he had always lectured and they soon let him know that they wanted things as they had always been. The experiment was a flop. It need not have been had there been proper preparation.

Since the teacher was apparently a strong Bible teacher and lecturer, it might have been better to continue lecturing. Principles and illustrations from the book would have enriched his lectures. From time to time, the teacher could ask a thought-provoking question and ask volunteers to express their opinions and experiences. Occasionally, the class could take time out to pray and to put into practice principles being taught. They could pray as a class or in groups of two or three for specific requests.

Use your imagination, be creative, and use variety to keep a class interesting and educational.

Far more Sunday school teachers of adults and teens are now using discussion, either as the basic teaching method or interspersed through lecture, than a few years ago. And people like it. It gives them a chance to come to grips with questions and problems for which they want answers. But if they are unaccustomed to participating in the learning process, use patience, imagination, variety and ingenuity. Someone has well said that small group discussion without preparation becomes a "pooling of ignorance."

Question-and-Answer or Parables?

Start with a question here and there during the lesson. Plan questions ahead of time. Do not ask one particular person a deep theological question. If he does not know the answer, he might be embarrassed or angry at being singled out.

Ask an opinion question: "Could we have some ideas about what we learn from the story of the widow's mite? Bill, would you care to start?" If the class is not accustomed to speaking up, prompt them: "Since our attention is on the widow, we would like to hear some opinions from the ladies. Can some of you identify with the tension created by this woman's financial straits and her desire to give to the Lord?"

At another point, ask, "Harry, looking at Jesus' focus on the Pharisees, how would you as a businessman apply the lesson to present-day society?"

Do not overdo it. If discussion is new to the class, wean them from total dependence on the lecture method a bit at a time. Ask for wisdom (James 1:5). Even occasional questions keep a class alert and thinking with the teacher.

In our family's devotions I learned not to ask my son, "Steve, how does this apply to you?" Children tend to feel uncomfortable with a question that is too personal. Instead, I would ask, "Steve, what do you think ten-year-old boys can learn from this Bible story?" This less-direct approach works better with adults as well!

Jesus taught the multitudes, but some of His most heart-searching questions were posed to a little group of twelve. Sometimes they were rhetorical questions (needing no verbal answers). "Jesus asked, 'You of little faith, why are you talking among yourselves about having no bread? Do you still not understand? Don't you remember the five loaves for the five thousand, and how many basketfuls you gathered? Or the seven loaves for the four thousand, and how many basketfuls you gathered? How is it you don't understand that I was not talking to you about bread? But be on your guard against the yeast of the Pharisees and Sadducees.' Then they understood" (Matthew 16:8-12).

Immediately following these verses are questions that did require answers. Jesus asked, "Who do people say the Son of Man is?" "But what about you? Who do you say I am?" (Matthew 16:13, 15). Although He asked the group, Peter alone volunteered an answer.

Jesus could be very direct in private. He asked the man born blind, whom He had healed, "Do you believe in the Son of Man?" (John 9:35).

He sometimes used a question to answer a question. "'By what authority are you doing these things' they asked. 'And who gave you this authority?' Jesus replied, 'I will also ask you one question....John's baptism—where did it come from? Was it from heaven, or from men?'" (Matthew 21:23-24).

In His parables, notice how He sprinkled questions here and there: "What do you think?" "Have you never read in the Scriptures...?" "You hypocrites, why are you trying to trap me?" "Whose portrait is this? And whose inscription?" "What do you think about the Christ? Whose son is he?" "How is it then that David, speaking by the Spirit, calls him 'Lord'?" "If then David calls him 'Lord,' how can he be his son?" (Selected from Matthew 21, 22.) Well-placed questions awaken people to think. Questions that motivate thought without the need of a reply, questions that demand an answer, questions that encourage discussion, questions that shut the mouths of the enemies of Christ—this is teaching at its finest!

No, teaching is not merely telling. Although the Master Teacher often said authoritatively, "I tell you the truth," He involved His hearers by motivating them to think.

Discussion or "The Way We've Always Done It"?

Jesus drew people into discussion. I can not think of a time when He asked a dead-end question—one that did not lead into deeper thought, require an answer, or expose evil in men's hearts. The best, most profound, and most enduring learning takes place when people discover truth for themselves, draw biblical conclusions and accept it as applicable to themselves.

Discussion takes place better in circles of seven or eight people who are facing each other. Pews are deadening to discussion; it is difficult to discuss anything with another person's back! When the group reaches ten, form another circle. The following diagrams illustrate the difference between discussion groups and other groups.

Lecture Method
(Leader does most of the talking.)

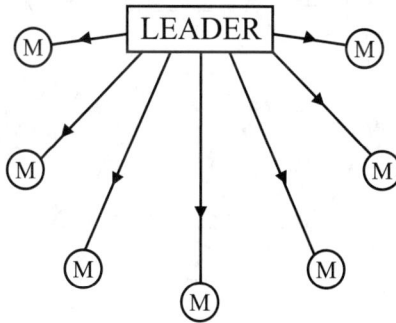

Question-and-Answer Method
(Leader asks; group members answer.)

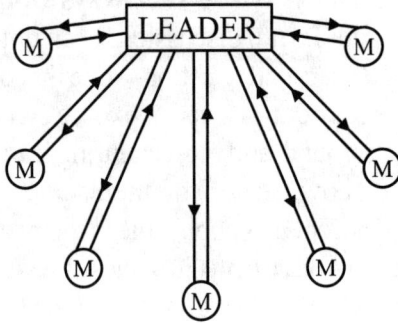

Discussion Method
(Leader begins discussion—perhaps with a question.
The leader functions as a member of the group,
not as the one who has all the answers.)

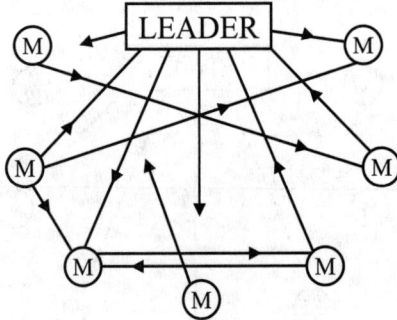

In discussion, the leader may draw others in with questions and may comment or offer his opinion. The leader encourages the group's spontaneous comments and their suggestions of appropriate Scripture, illustrations, and applications. Members offer ideas and opinions, ask questions and respond to each other. If a question is directed to the Leader, he may answer or redirect the question to someone else. It is his responsibility to keep the discussion on track. He is not afraid to say, "I don't know. Who will see what you can find out and report to us next time? Where can you find help?" The leader should also politely keep anyone from monopolizing the discussion. He or she can say, "Thank you, Frank, for those insights. Jane, do you know of any case that would illustrate this truth?" Contrary to the opinion of some who think discussion is not really teaching, it can be masterful teaching if one thinks of teaching as guiding the learner in the discovery of truth.

In the preceding section of this chapter, under the heading, Question-and-Answer, we noticed that questions motivate discussion. True. But not all questions. Questions that generate truth-discovering discussion often begin with the words *who, what, when, where, why,* and *how.* Questions that merely call for factual answers or that can be answered with a *yes* or a *no* are dead-end questions. The discussion won't go anywhere. When someone answers a question of that sort, it concludes the matter. Use questions that draw people out, that solicit their opinions or ideas. If you do ask a question that can be answered with a *yes* or *no,* follow it with, "Why do you feel as you do?" Or, "Would you care to explain your answer?"

Either-Or or Both-And?

Jesus was not confined to the speech to inform or the speech to persuade. In fact, I have an idea that some folks were entertained and others startled half out of their wits when He called the religious big shots "whited sepulchers full of dead men's bones." Nor did He restrict Himself to preaching or discussion or question-and-answer. He used them all. Often, He used startling statements that shook both Pharisees and disciples out of their ritualistic ruts. He asked questions to expose hypocrisy. But He also used them to draw people toward the right conclusion. Among the times He used the lecture method were His best-known Sermon on the Mount (Matthew 5-7) and His Upper Room Discourse (John 14-16). Yet, He frequently brought others into the discussion to drive home a point.

What do *you* think? What kind of teaching is the most challenging? Which stimulates us to search the Scriptures? Which motivates an active behavioral response? Which causes us to face up to our sins and failures and the realization that we must give an answer to God Himself?

Is it really either/or? Should I ask, "Which method should I use?" Or should I pray, "Lord, teach me to follow the Master Teacher's example in using a variety of methods effectively"? Consider also the most appropriate methods for the age of the class members. How blest we are when a teacher targets and holds our attention on the Word of the Living God and sends us forth to obey it!

CHAPTER 5

Outline Your Talk

An outline is a chart to organize your ideas so you can share them easily. Or it can be thought of as a map to help people follow your thoughts. When the road divides, to arrive at your desired destination by the most direct route, consult your map. Not to do so would be to waste time, energy, and fuel—and risk failing to arrive at your destination. Just so, to reach your desired conclusion when speaking, follow a clear outline. Without it, you might wander and not accomplish your aim.

Think of a speech as a tree with limbs, branches, leaves and fruit. The leaves and fruit must be supported and fed by the branches. The branches grow out of the limbs, which grow from the trunk, which must be rooted securely in the earth.

The *roots* represent your studying in preparation for your devotional talk, lesson or sermon. They anchor the talk firmly in God's Word and draw truth from it to nourish the trunk, the limbs, the branches, the leaves and the fruit.

The *trunk* is your topic (theme), such as one of the following: The Love of God, heaven, hell, or the Virgin Birth of Christ.

Heavier *limbs* growing out of the trunk are the main divisions of the outline.

The *branches* are subdivisions.

The Outline As a Tree

(The Trunk: Title)

How To Be Saved and Show It
Ephesians 2:8-10

(Limb: **Main Division**)

1. Salvation: Given by Grace

(Branches: Subdivisions)

A. Grace: undeserved favor

B. Grace: free gift

(Limb: **Main Division**)

2. Salvation: Received through Faith

(Branches: Subdivisions)

A. Faith: trust with certainty.

B. Faith: confidence in God's Word

(Limb: **Main Division**)

3. Salvation: Not Earned by Works

A. If by works, it would not be *free grace*.

(Branches: Subdivisions)

B. If by works, it would not be *simple faith*.

C. If by works, it would not be *God's glory*.

(Limb: **Main Division**)

4. Salvation: Produces Good Works

A. God created us anew in Christ to do good works.

(Branches: Subdivisions)

B. He prepared good works in advance for us to do.

Leaves and fruit cover limbs and branches. The audience enjoys the fruit of your study; they do not have to be aware of the outline, the structure beneath the message. However, some folks appreciate a printed outline of the sermon to help them take notes.

Other Illustrations: How Outlines Work

A pastor boasted, "I don't use an outline. I just get up and preach." He did not stay with any church very long. Such bragging is of the flesh, not the Spirit. A public speaker must have something worth saying. He or she must say it in a way that people will understand and know how to apply it. An outline arranges thoughts so they will flow logically and can be easily followed. Following, I've listed useful ways to think of an outline.

A building. How is an outline like the steel skeletal structure of a building? What do the invisible steel girders accomplish? Are people who see or enter the building necessarily aware of the girders?

The human body. What part of the human body would you compare with the outline of a talk? Why?

An airplane. How would an airplane get off the ground if its builder had no design for the basic structure of the fuselage, airfoils and engine? As an airline pilot and a surgeon have peoples' lives in their hands so a Christian speaker has the gospel that determines eternal destiny. If we expect a pilot to follow charts and radio signals, shouldn't we, who have the message of eternal life, have a clear plan?

A child's blocks. A child soon learns that he cannot pile his toy blocks just any way with no plan or they will fall. The parts of an outline are like a stack of toy blocks. The theme, the main idea of your message, gives

unity to the speech.
Outline divisions, like
building blocks, build
toward the aim (goal).

A workman's tool:
There are correct tools
to use for specific jobs.
A mechanic does not
often use an adjustable
wrench; he prefers a
wrench that is the exact size to fit each bolt or nut.

A good outline is the right tool for a speaker. It is easy to use.
Do not clutter your notes; leave enough white space so the outline
parts are easy to see at a glance while speaking. You may use any
gimmicks you wish to make it easier to read it at a glance while
keeping eye contact. Some gimmicks you may use are the following:

ALL CAPITAL LETTERS, **BOLD LETTERS,** *Italics,*
special indention, highlight, a box drawn around the words . You
are free to underline, use [brackets], (parentheses), symbols such
as &, /, #, %, @, ~, =, or anything that is meaningful to *you.* You
probably will not use many symbols, but you may use them when
they help you to see at a glance something to remind you of what
you want to say while maintaining good eye contact with your
listeners. Your outline for speaking is *your* tool, not an assignment
following all the rules of grammar to please someone else.

As you get experience speaking from an outline, you will
develop ways of making it more useful. Use your own shorthand.
I use w. for the word *with,* pr for *prayer* and PTL! for *Praise the
Lord!* A capital F is all right for *God the Father,* but be careful
because H. S. might register in your mind as *Holy Spirit* when
you mean *high school.* If two levels are enough to remind you of
the thoughts you studied and want to teach or preach, don't use
three or four levels. A long outline with long, run-on sentences,
whole paragraphs or too many levels is like a cheap, dull tool.

Parts of an Outline

The theme. The theme is the basic *thought* of the message, the Bible truth that the speaker must explain clearly. It is the idea in mind throughout the talk. It guides the speaker in preparing the outline. Although not something announced or advertised, it is basic to planning the outline. Keep your *aim* in mind throughout as you develop your theme. Omit any stories and thoughts that do not add anything to your aim. If they do not contribute, they detract from the truth you are developing.

The title. Suggest the idea of the theme in a short title to catch people's attention and create interest.

The main divisions. Each main division (1., 2., 3., and perhaps more) says something important about the theme.

The subdivisions. Subdivisions follow main divisions. Each subdivision says something about its main division.

An outline for a Bible lesson, sermon or devotional talk may have the theme, "God's plan of eternal redemption for all mankind." However, a theme is not a title. This theme can be better expressed in a short title: *God's Plan for Man.* The theme is not actually a part of the outline; it is the thought behind the outline. The first part of the outline is the title. In the following outline identify: *title*, *main divisions* and *subdivisions*. Notice how each main division relates to the theme and how each subdivision relates to its main division.

God's Eternal Plan (Ephesians 1:10-11; Isaiah 14:26-27)

1. **The Origin of God's Eternal Plan**
   A. God's Heart (John 3:16)
   B. God's Person (Eph. 1:4-9)

2. **The Objective of God's Eternal Plan**
   A. Christ: provider of salvation for all mankind (Rom.10:12,13)
   B. Christians: messengers to all mankind (Mark 15:16)

3. The Outcome of God's Eternal Plan

    A. Overview of History (man's story)

        (1) Genesis 1, 2 (only 2 chapters) tell man's **PRE-SIN** history.

        (2) Genesis 3–Revelation 20 (all except four chapters of the Bible) tell man's **SIN** history.

        (3) Revelation 21, 22 (only two chapters) tell man's **POST-SIN** history.

Illustration (a timeline):

Man's History

Pre-Sin	**Sin**	**Post-Sin**
(Gen. 1-2)	**(Gen. 3-Rev. 20)**	**(Rev. 21-22)**

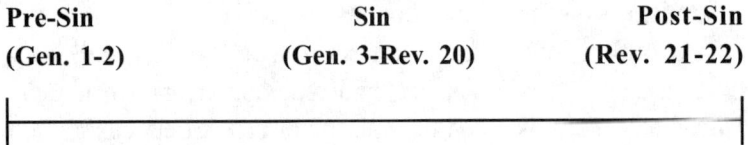

    B. Overview of Scripture

        (1) Old Testament: drawing the nations to God through Israel (Exodus 19:5-6; Isaiah 27:12-13)

        (2) New Testament: sending the Church into all the world (Matthew 28:18-20; Ephesians 2:15-17; 3:10-12)

    C. Triumph of the Gospel

    (*Read* Revelation 5:9-11; Revelation 22:17, 20 without comment.)

The general appearance: Notice how the outline above keeps the parts of the outline straight with their similar parts; **1, 2,** and **3** are in a straight vertical line so you recognize them as main divisions. **A, B,** and **C** are indented but aligned with each other so they are recognizable as subdivisions. A second line of any division should be indented so that it falls in line with the wording directly above it. A well-laid-out outline is much easier to use and helps the speaker to hold the attention of the listeners.

CHAPTER 6

Outline Your Topic

Here is an example of a simple topical outline. The theme or topic, "what the Bible teaches about the person and work of Jesus Christ," is too long and involved to be a good title. A better title is Who Is Jesus Christ?

Topical Outline

(Title)   **WHO IS JESUS CHRIST?**

(Three   1. He is the Son of God. (Matthew 14:33)
Main   2. He is the Son of Man. (Matthew 8:20)
Divisions)   3. He is the Savior of the World. (1 John 4:14)

In a topical outline the topic is the main truth of the speech. That makes it different from a textual outline, in which the main idea is set fort in a single text. Every main division of the topical outline contributes something to the topic. At least one text (Bible verse) supports each main division and may be chosen from any part of the Bible. Look up each verse in the outline above. Does it teach what its main division says? Does each main division help to answer the question in the title and thereby contribute to the topic?

When you use a topical message, be careful to use Scripture wisely and not merely to defend your own ideas. That is, make sure that all divisions and supporting verses are true to the overall teaching and emphasis of Scripture. Do not ignore the context of the verse in seeking a verse to support your outline.

Textual Outline

The textual outline explains and applies the truth in a single text of one or two verses. Although other verses may be used to reinforce thoughts, the main divisions of the outline must all come from truths within the text itself. Look at Romans 12:1-2 as an example: "Therefore, I urge you, brothers, in view of God's mercy, to offer your bodies as living sacrifices, holy and pleasing to God—this is your spiritual act of worship. Do not conform any longer to the pattern of this world, but be transformed by the renewing of your mind. Then you will be able to test and approve what God's will is—his good, pleasing and perfect will."

(Title)	**A LIVING SACRIFICE**
(Text)	Romans 12:1-2
(Three Main Divisions)	1. Offering Your Body
	2. Refusing to Conform
	3. Renewing Your Mind

Do you find each of these divisions clearly in the text? The very words do not have to be in the text, but the truths indicated by the divisions must be clear and entirely from the text. A textual outline is easy for the speaker to use and the congregation to follow. The text is easy to understand because the main divisions point out important truths in it. It is also easier than a topical message for people to follow in their Bibles.

However, there is no one way that is the only correct way to outline a text. Romans 12:1-2, above, could be outlined as follows:

1. Heeding the appeal for a living sacrifice (v. 1)
2. Obeying the command to be transformed (v. 2a)
3. Approving God's will for your life (v. 2b)

Again, using important words in the verses to guide us, it might be quite different:

1. Mercy of God
2. Sacrifice of our bodies
3. Act of Worship
4. Conformity to the world
5. Transformation by mental renewing

A textual outline also helps us to stick to the Bible. We are not as tempted to use Scripture to support our own notions as we might be in a topical outline. We will study textual outlines in more detail in later chapters.

Expository Outline (explaining a longer passage of Scripture)

(Title)	**THE LIVING WORD**
(Text)	John 1:1-18
(Three Main Divisions)	1. The eternal Word (verses 1-5) 2. The God-sent witness (verses 6-8, 15-18) 3. The enfleshed Word (verses 9-14)

In the above outline, you could use the word *incarnate* instead of *enfleshed*, but often people who have heard the word *incarnate* for years do not know what it means. When you read verse 14, "And the Word became flesh," *enfleshed* becomes more meaningful: the Word in human flesh.

The expository outline takes all its main divisions from one Scripture passage longer than that used in a textual outline. Although either the topical message or the textual message can be useful on occasion, Bible teachers regularly rely on the expository approach to go deeper into God's Word. This is the kind of message a pastor should preach regularly. It builds up the believers in their Bible knowledge. The expository outline helps to keep our thoughts on what *God* is saying to us instead of trying to prove *our* point. Several chapters will be devoted to this method, so we will not include a detailed outline here.

Keeping Outlines for Future Use

Keep your outlines. You may use them again sometime for a different class or congregation, or they will be seed-plots to help you develop new talks. For the outlines you wish to file for future reference print sentences in full. If you use only phrases or key words, you may not remember fully what your thoughts were when you want to modify an outline or use it again. You may think you will never forget the ideas that are so important to you now, but you will! You may also want to keep the five-inch by eight-inch cards for your preaching or teaching outlines

Use a sturdy box; and store it in a dry place. Make two parts:
(1) Outlines filed by **Text**
(2) Outlines filed by **Topic**

Filing by Text

Put the outlines in folders. In the first part, arrange outlines in the order the texts appear in the Bible.

GEN. - DEUT.	JOSHUA - RUTH	1 SAM. - 2 CHR.

EZRA - JOB	PSALMS	PROV. - ECCL.

Filing by Topic

In the second part of your file box, or in another box, arrange the outlines in alphabetical order by topic as in the following folders:

ABRAHAM	BLOOD	CROSS

Speaking from Your Outline

The outline you use for speaking may be different from the one you file for future use. As previously mentioned, short sentences, phrases or words that remind you of the complete thought at a glance make it easier to speak while keeping eye contact. Type or print neatly.

Use five-inch by eight-inch index cards when speaking. You can buy them at stores that sell office supplies. They do not distract people's attention. You can keep these cards in your Bible until you are ready to speak. They lie flat and will not blow away in wind from an open window or fan.

The Modified Outline

Speak from the kind of outline that ties you to your audience, not to your notes. A few preachers can read a sermon well, but they often have difficulty keeping eye contact for personal communication. Which of the following outlines will make it easier to think on your feet so you can speak from your heart and not merely read your notes?

Lengthy Sentence Outline

1. We must always remember that Jesus Christ is the very Son of God Almighty, Creator of Heaven and Earth.

2. Let us also remember that He is the Son of Man, who was tempted in all points like we are.

3. Because Jesus was the Son of God and the Son of Man, He was uniquely qualified to be the Savior of the World.

To make the above outline easier to read, use condensed sentences.

Condensed Sentence Outline

1. Jesus Christ is the Son of God.

2. Jesus Christ is the Son of Man.

3. Jesus Christ is the Savior of the world.

This one is easy to use, but it can be condensed to single phrases without losing any important information.

Single Phrase Outline

Jesus Christ

1. Son of God

2. Son of Man

3. Savior of the World

Phrases are even easier to see at a glance.

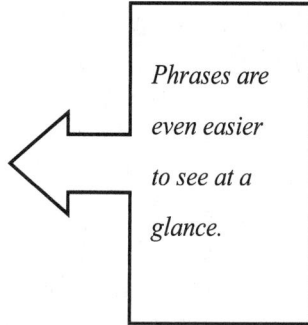

Dr. Ted S. Rendall, chancellor and retired president of Prairie Bible Institute, used short sentences in the outline below. Because the personal assurance in each statement answers the question in the title, these short sentences are more effective than phrases.

.

VICTORY—FOR ME?

1. YES! You Can Have Victory Over Every Sin.
Rom. 5:17; 6:14; 7:24, 25.
(See Mic. 7:19, and pray Ps. 119:133.)

2. YES! You Can Have Victory Over Every Circumstance.
2 Cor. 2:14; Phil. 4:10-13.

3. YES! You Can Have Victory Over Every Crisis.
Rom. 8:31-39.

Hymnals and holidays provide ideas for topics and texts. Easter, Mother's Day, Father's Day, Thanksgiving, and Christmas suggest good ideas. Attention is focused on these celebrations.[11] Keep a list of topics from your daily Bible reading, the news, nature, and other sources as you think of them. I have listed some possible topics to help you get started.

Some Topics for Outlines

The Way of Salvation	Redeemed By the Blood
Angels	A Prayer for Revival
The Light of the World	Spiritual Warfare
Which Master ?	The Great Commission
The Wise and the Foolish	Fishers of Men
Thanksgiving	Temptation
The Greatest Gift	Effective Prayer
Alone With God	Names of God
The True Tabernacle	Names and Titles of Jesus
Rest for the Weary	Victory in Jesus
The Kingdom of God	The Word of God
Sin and Salvation	The Glory of God
Heaven	The Judgment Bar of God
Holiness	Hell
The Final War	Freedom Not to Sin
Truth	Justified!
Mother	The Meaning of the Cross
Christ In You	The Prince of Peace
Knowing God	The Resurrection
The Family	The Resurrected Life
Abiding in Christ	Mountain Peaks
Access to God	The Authority of Christ
Son of God/Son of Man	In Jesus' Name, Amen!
A Light in a Dark Place	Honor Father & Mother

Attributes of God, such as the following, are good topics:

Omnipresence	Omnipotence	Omniscience
Holiness	Truth	Eternity
Goodness	Justice	Mercy
Faithfulness	Grace	Love
Righteousness	Immutability	Loving-kindness
Transcendence		

CHAPTER 7

Do It Yourself

It is time to make your own outline. *Use your Bible.* This chapter will guide you in developing an outline to use for an evangelistic emphasis in a devotional talk, Bible study, or sermon.

Preparing to Choose a Theme

Begin your preparation by prayerfully deciding what the theme will be. Some important matters to consider are these:

1. What is the occasion?

Holiday?	Business persons' lunch?
Graduation?	Mid-week prayer meeting?
Funeral?	Sunday morning worship service?
Youth meeting?	Home Bible study?
Men's breakfast?	Devotional talk?
Sunday school class?	VBS final program?

2. What can I expect my audience to be like?

    Will they be adults, teens, or children?
    Will they be men, women, or both?
    Should I expect all believers or some unsaved?

3. What are their special needs?

Salvation?   Spiritual growth?
Companionship?   Encouragement?
Comfort?   Motivation to service?

4. Is it a group with special interests?

A Boy Scout troop?   A seniors' home?
A missionary society?   A high school chapel?
A children's camp?   A city rescue mission?
A refugee camp?   A team of Christian athletes?
A pre-evangelistic campaign rally?

Choosing a Theme (Practice Theme #1)

Read the following verses:
Ex. 12:22   Matt. 26:28
Rom. 3:25   Rev. 5:9
Rom. 5:9   Eph. 1:7
Col. 1:20   Rev. 7:14
Heb. 9:7, 12-14   1 Peter 1:18-19
1 John 1:7

From the verses above, what one word can you fill in for each of the suggested themes that follow? (Use the same word for all blanks.)

- The Sacrifice of _____
- Salvation by the _____
- Faith in Jesus' Shed _____
- Justified by the _____ of Christ
- The _____ of the Lamb
- Christ's _____ Shed for Sinners
- Reconciled to God through Jesus' Shed _____

From the list , select the theme that you prefer (or write your own).

Choosing Another Theme (Practice Theme #2)

Suppose that you are going to speak to a family gathering of men, women, and children. Some are Christians, but some may not yet have been born again by faith in Jesus Christ. You will want to select a theme to point the unsaved to Him for salvation. However, you will also need to help believers of all ages appreciate the salvation Christ has given them.

After studying the following verses and answering the questions briefly, complete the sentence below the questions:

Rom. 3:23   Who has sinned?
Rom. 6:23   What is sin's payment?
1 Tim. 1:15   Whom did the Lord Jesus come to save?

Salvation is for _____.

The short preceding sentence could be completed with the general word *everybody*. However, the more specific word *sinners* would be better for the theme of this message, because it tells the particular thought in all the verses. Therefore, the theme is: Salvation is for *sinners*.

Your outline can develop the theme in the following ways:
• It may explain what the theme means.
• It may prove that the theme is true.
• It may persuade people to apply the truth by confessing their sinfulness and receiving Christ.
• It may encourage Christians to thank the Lord for His great salvation.

Deciding on Main Divisions

Each main division must say something important about the theme. Complete one main division for each verse:

1. All people have _____ (Rom. 3:23).
2. The payment for sin is _____ (Rom. 6:23a).
3. The gift of God is _____ life (Rom. 6:23b).
4. Christ Jesus came to _____ _____ (I Tim. 1:15).

Be sure each main division does two things:
- First, it must declare the truth in the verse.
- Second, it must support (or develop) the theme.

TIP:

Main divisions may be related to the theme in several ways:

They may *explain* something about the theme.

Taken together, the main divisions *develop* the theme step by step.

In other outlines, main divisions may *defend* the theme or *support* the theme with evidence.

Using Subdivisions

Subdivisions explain each main division or support it with evidence or arguments

THEME		
MAIN DIVISION 1	**MAIN DIVISION 2**	**MAIN DIVISION 3**
SUBDIVISIONS	*SUBDIVISIONS*	*SUBDIVISIONS*
A **B**	**A** **B** **C**	**A** **B**

Choosing the Title

A brief title may be used to announce the message for a newspaper, radio or poster. The title may be the same as the theme if the theme is short and if the title does the following three things:

- Suggest the idea of the theme.
- Attract attention.
- Create interest in the message.

When you have chosen your theme, you may decide on a title, or you may prefer to choose the title at some time later in your study. Often, you may have a clearer idea how you want to word a title as you prepare the parts of the outline. Remember that the title should suggest the theme, but it should not present the whole idea that you will develop in the speech.

CHAPTER **8**

Continue Your Own Outline

Beginning with practice theme #2 in chapter seven as your example, make a copy of the outline below and fill in the blanks. You may choose the title either before or after you finish the outline.

Title: _____

1. **All people have** _____ (Rom. 3:23).
   A.   _____ and ____ sinned (Gen. 3).
   B.   _____ sinned (Gen. 4).
   C.   King _____ sinned (Ps. 51:3-5).
   D.   _____ sinned (1 Tim. 1:1, 15).
   E.   _____ sinned (Isa. 53:6; Ps. 53:3; Rom. 3:12).

2. **The payment for sin is** _____ (Rom. 6:23a).
   A.   Ezek. 18:20: The soul that _____ will _____.
   B.   Rev. 21:8: Sinners will experience the "second _____".

3. **The Gift of God is** _____ ____ (Romans 6:23b).
   A.   Jesus Christ is the way, the truth and the _____ (John 14:6; John 1:4).
   B.   God gave His Son so that all who believe in Him can have _____ _____ (John 3:16).

    C.   By receiving the Son we receive
_____ _____ (John 3:36).

4. Christ Jesus came to _____ sinners (1 Tim. 1:15).
  A. _____
      (John 3:16-17).
  B. _____
      (Acts 16:31).
  C. _____
      (Rev. 22:17; John 1:12).

Write a short *sentence* for each of the three subdivisions under Number 4, above. Each should tell the most important thought of the verse or verses. Now, you have a two-level outline. The first level is indicated by the numbered points, the second level by the letters.

Find Verses

Suppose, as you prayerfully study for a talk, the Holy Spirit reminds you of the importance of the shed blood of the Savior and you think of Romans 5:9, "…we have now been justified by his blood…." You realize you need to read more on the topic of the shed blood of Christ.

If you have center-column references in your Bible or notes at the bottom of each page, they may lead you to more verses on the topic. If you have a concordance in the back of your Bible, study it to find verses on a topic. Look up the key word: *blood*. With a larger concordance such as *Strong's*, *Young's* or *Cruden's*, you can look up verses for any word in the Bible.

Other Bible-study helps that are especially useful for preparing topical sermons are *The Thompson Chain Reference Bible*, *Monser's Topical Index and Digest of the Bible* and *The Treasury of Scripture Knowledge*. Your church librarian, pastor, or missionary, can help you find out where to get such books. Several good Bible programs are available on the Internet with concordances and topical indexes. Search under *Bible* or *Bible Study*.

LEARN FROM SAMPLE OUTLINES

We will now study an example of a good topical outline. Later, we will contrast the good outline to poor outlines. Study the Bible verses to understand how the theme, the title and the body of the outline were chosen and developed.

VERSES TO STUDY

Isaiah 7:14   Micah 5:2   Matt. 1:18-24
Matt. 2:1-12   Luke 2:1-7   Luke 2:8-20
John 1:1-18   John 3:16

Sample Outline
The theme, *Jesus was born to be the Savior of the world*, is the thought that is to be carried throughout the outline, but it is not a part of the outline.

(Title) **The Savior of the World**

(Body) 1. The Savior's birth was prophesied hundreds of years before Jesus Christ was born (Isaiah 7:14; Micah 5:2).
2. Jesus Christ's birth fulfilled the prophecies about the birth of the Savior (Matthew 1:18-24; Luke 2:1-7).
3. Jesus' birth was God's plan from the beginning (John 1:1-18).
4. God's purpose in Jesus' birth was to provide a Savior for us (John 3:16).

You may use topical messages for special occasions. The preceding outline would be a good one to use during the Christmas season. However, it is *always* timely to speak about the Savior of the world and to invite people to receive Him. Any believer who speaks to a group can use it anytime for God's glory.

Write the Conclusion

To close your message, you need a strong conclusion. Do not introduce new thoughts in the conclusion. You may use it to *summarize* the main divisions in the body of the message and to *apply* it to the lives of those present. Here is a good conclusion for the preceding outline: As God planned from the beginning, Jesus Christ fulfilled the prophecies about the Savior of the world. He is God's gift to us. Will you receive Him now?

Make the Outline Simple

Since you will shorten your speaking outline from the complete-sentence outline you design to file, this section helps you to shorten your outline. With use, you will find the kind of outline that is easiest for *you* to use.

Instead of long sentences, use shorter sentences:

1. God gave prophecies (Isa. 7:14; Mic.5:2).
2. God fulfilled prophecies (Matt. 1:18-24; Luke 2:1-7).
3. God revealed His plan (John 1:1-18).
4. God declared His purpose (John 3:16).

Or you may use phrases:

1. Prophecies given (Isa. 7:14; Mic.5:2)
2. Prophecies fulfilled (Matt. 1:18-24; Luke 2:1-7)
3. Plan revealed (John 1:1-18)
4. Purpose declared (John 3:16)

To make it simpler yet, combine *Prophecies given* and *Prophecies fulfilled* into one: *Prophecies*. Reduce the outline to three one-word main divisions:

1. Prophecies
   (Isa. 7:14; Matt. 1:18-24; Mic.5:2; Luke 2:1-7)
2. Plan (John 1:1-18)
3. Purpose (John 3:16)

One word for a main division is sometimes enough to remind you of the entire idea, and you can easily memorize the three main divisions.

The first main division can be divided into these subdivisions:

1. Prophecies
   A. Prophecies given (Isaiah 7:14; Micah 5:2).
   B. Prophecies fulfilled (Matthew 1:18-24; Luke 2:1-7).

The advantages of making the outline simpler are:

- reading division headings at a glance;
- keeping good eye contact with your listeners.

Dr. Bryan Chapell says, "A speaker who will not look people in the eyes is deemed aloof, afraid, and/or incompetent. You must look at people! When you deny people your eyes, you really deny them yourself."[12] This is true in all except a very few cultures in the world.

CHAPTER 9

Follow a Logical Pattern

The purpose of an outline is to make it easy to give a speech and to understand it. A balanced outline is important.

Make all main divisions of an outline alike:

* **If you use *sentences*, make them simple and clear.**
* **If you use *phrases*, use only phrases, not sentences, for all main divisions.**
* **If you use *a single word* for one main division, use only one word for each main division.**

The style balances the outline. Balanced divisions do not always have the same number of words. A prepositional phrase in one main division may have three words ("in God's Word"). In the next main division the prepositional phrase may have more words ("on the Sea of Galilee") or fewer ("for God"). The fact that they are all prepositional phrases balances the outline.

You may use different styles for different outlines—sentences for the main divisions of one outline, phrases for another outline, and single words for another. But using only one style for all the main divisions of the same outline makes it easier for the speaker and his listeners to keep the main thoughts in mind. We learn much better when the thoughts are presented in an orderly and logical fashion.

You may use different styles on different levels. That is, you may use one style for main divisions and another style for subdivisions. For instance, main divisions may be sentences and subdivisions may be phrases. However, you should keep *all parts of any one level the same*. This balance makes the outline easy to follow; it is worth the extra effort.

Chronological Order

We can follow a speaker whose thoughts are in chronological order, the order in which events happened—the order of time.

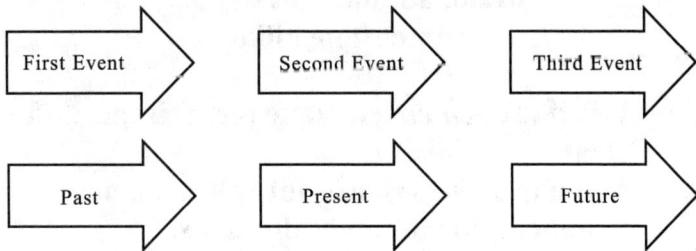

First Event	Second Event	Third Event
Past	Present	Future

A logical arrangement of divisions follows:
1. Purpose for all mankind (John 3:16)
2. Plan from the beginning (John 1:1-18)
3. Prophecies of Christ's coming (Isaiah 7:14; Micah 5:2)
4. Fulfillment of Messianic prophecies
   (Matt. 1:18-24; Luke 2:1-7)

Cause and Effect

We can easily follow thoughts in a *cause-and-effect* order, an action (cause) followed by the results of that action (effect).

CAUSE: "All have sinned" (Romans 3:23).
EFFECT: "The wages of sin is death" (Romans 6:23).

Notice John 3:16:

(CAUSE)   "For God so loved the world"
(EFFECT)   "that He gave His one and only Son."

[This effect then becomes a cause of the next effect.]

(CAUSE)   "He gave His one and only Son"
(EFFECT)   "that whoever believes in Him shall not
             perish but have eternal life."

Comparison

Jesus often used comparisons in His teaching. One chapter, Matthew 13, provides several examples.

In the parable of the farmer and the seed, Jesus used metaphors for making comparisons. A metaphor compares two things by saying, "This is that." He compared the seed with the Word of God ("this is the seed"), and He compared the soil conditions where the seed fell with men who hear the Word of God with different reactions. The seed snatched away by the evil one "is the seed sown along the path." The seed sown on rocky places is "the man who hears the word and at once receives it with joy. But since he has no root, he lasts only a short time." The seed among thorns is "the man who hears the word, but the worries of this life and the deceitfulness of wealth choke it." "But the one who received the seed that fell on good soil is the man who hears the word and understands it. He produces a crop, yielding a hundred, sixty or thirty times what was sown."

In the next parable of Matthew 13, the parable of the weeds, Jesus used similes for comparisons. A simile does not say, "This *is* that," but "This is *like* that." "The kingdom of heaven is like a man who sowed good seed in his field." He also said, "The kingdom of heaven is like a mustard seed," and, "The kingdom of heaven is like yeast."

In His explanation of the parable of the weeds to the disciples He went back to the use of metaphors, "The one who sowed the good seed is the Son of Man. The field is the world."

Comparisons by the use of metaphors or similes help us to see pictures in our minds. This is a good device for a teacher to use.

Contrast

Still another logical order shows contrast. Look at Psalm 1. Use your open Bible to understand the lesson.

Psalm 1:

Verses 1-3: The Blessed Man

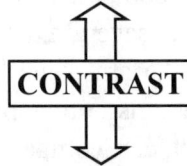

⇑

CONTRAST

⇓

Verses 4 and 5: The Wicked Man

Verse 6: Summary—
The Blessed & The Wicked

Question-and-Answer

The next outline follows question-and-answer logic. Although one of the ways question-and-answer may be used is in the discussion, it is effective in a variety of public speaking styles. In the next outline each *main division* gives an answer to the question, "Why does God give us prophecy?"

The Significance of End-Time Prophecies

Introduction: Prophecy is important to us.

1. **Evidence of prophecy's importance from Scripture:**

   A. Books called "The Books of Prophecy" account for more than ¼ of the Bible.

   B. There are other prophetic books:
   1, 2 Thessalonians; 1, 2 Peter; Jude.

   C. There are also many texts such as:
   Genesis 3:15; 12:1-3; Matthew 1-4; Matthew 28:20; John 14:2,3; Titus 2:13; I John 3:2,3.

2. **Evidence from world events:** Matthew 24:33-34

   A. 1900-2000: Two world wars (first "world" wars in history)

   B. Worst famines in history; increasing; millions of lives lost

   C. More severe and more frequent earthquakes (US Geological Survey statistics)

   D. Plagues; space phenomena; the return of Jews to their homeland, apostasy, technology and the means to reach the world with the gospel in this generation

3. God's purpose in giving us prophecy

A. To turn people from sin to the Savior
Jeremiah 36:3; 1 Thessalonians 5:2-3; 2 Peter 3:10

B. To strengthen our faith by confirming His Word—
Zechariah 2:8, 9; John 13:19; 14:29

Illustration:
Old Testament prophecies fulfilled in New Testament:
• Micah 5:2 (Christ born in Bethlehem)
• Isaiah 7:14 (Born of a virgin)
• Psalm 22; Isaiah 53 (Crucifixion)
• Zechariah 12:10 (Pierced)

C. To encourage faithfulness and steadfastness—
John 16:1 (context Jn. 15, 16: persecution, martyrdom)
John 16:2 (More martyrs today than ever before!)

D. To motivate holiness, sanctification, moral purity—
1 Thessalonians 3:13 through chapter 4:8;
Titus 2:12, 13; 1 John 3:3

E. To teach us to resist the devil, to be sober and vigilant and
to endure suffering patiently—1 Peter 5:8, 9

F. To motivate love for our brothers and sisters in Christ—
1 Thessalonians 3:12; 4:9, 10

G. To motivate us to encourage, edify and comfort one
another— 1 Thessalonians 4:18; 5:11

Subdivisions

We need more than one level to develop a complete outline. Main divisions are the first level. Divisions on the second level are called subdivisions. Subdivisions develop or support main divisions. They are indicated by A, B, C. Use letters for as many subdivisions as you need.

Following is the form of a topical outline with two levels:

(Level One)   1.   Main division

(Level Two)   A. Subdivision
                     B. Subdivision

(Level One)   2.   Main division

(Level Two)   A. Subdivision
                     B. Subdivision
                     C. Subdivision

In the next outline notice the balanced main divisions, numbered and in bold print (first level) and the balanced subdivisions, indicated with capital letters (second level).

The Most Important Time of Your Life: Now!
2 Corinthians 6:2

1. It is time to look back (Psalm 143:5).

    A. Time to remember (Psalm 105:5)
    B. Time to confess (1 John 1:9)
    C. Time to forsake sin (Isaiah 55:7a)
    D. Time to turn to God (Isaiah 55:7b)

2. It is time to look ahead (Psalm 48:14).

    A. Wake up! (Romans 13:11-14, especially v.11)
    B. Watch! (Mark 13:32-37, especially verses 32, 37)
    C. Obey! (Romans 1:5)

3. It is time to have a "heart purpose" (Dan. 1:8 KJV).

    A. To seek the Lord (Isaiah 55:6)
    B. To present your body to the Lord (Romans 12:1,2)
    C. To glorify God in all you do (1 Corinthians 10:31)

Conclusion:
    A. It is time to LOOK BACK:
        • *Remember* God's blessings.
        • *Confess* and *forsake* sin.
        • *Turn to God* fully in faith.
    B. It is time to LOOK AHEAD: *Wake up! Watch! Obey!*
    C. It is time to ESTABLISH your *"heart purpose."*

Notice that subdivisions under any one main division have the same style. However, subdivisions may have different styles from one main division to another.

- Main division 1 and 3 use *phrases* for their subdivisions.
- Main division 2 uses *brief commands* (imperative sentences) for its subdivisions.

If you prefer, for emphasis, you could use a longer phrase for each *subdivision* supporting main division 3.

    A. *A heart purpose* to seek the Lord.

    B. *A heart purpose* to present your body to the Lord.

    C. *A heart purpose* to glorify God in all you do.

The following expository outline has a different logical arrangement. The main divisions merely *list* two triumphs of the Lord and the subdivisions explain, illustrate or argue for them.

The Triumph of Jesus Christ, Jn. 12:12-50
(A Palm Sunday message)

Introduction:

Illustration: "Triumph"—a parade for a victorious Roman general.

Two ways Palm Sunday is a "triumph," a celebration of victory (John 12: 12:12-50)

1. The triumph of the prophecies of God (verse 16)

    A. These prophecies prove the inspiration of the Scriptures.

        (1) Verse 13 quotes Psalm 118:26.
        (2) Verses 14, 15 quote Zechariah 9:9.
        (3) Verses 32-33 and John 3:14 fulfill Numbers 21:7-9.
        (4) Verses 37-38 fulfill Isaiah 53:1 and Isaiah 6:10.

    B. This passage provides the revelation of the Savior.

        (1) Jewish disciples' belated revelation of Christ (v. 16)
        (2) Greeks' (Jewish proselytes from among the Gentiles) personal introduction to Jesus (vv. 20-22)
        (3) Isaiah's prophetic revelation of Jesus (John 12:38-41; Isaiah 6:10)

2. The triumph of the Prince of Glory

    A. Triumph of life over death

        (1) His "hour" (verses 23, 27-28)
        (2) His "glorification" (verses 23, 27-28a, 32-33, 41)

B. Triumph of light over darkness

   (1) Trust in the light (verses 35, 36).
   (2) Believe in Jesus Christ .
      (verse 46; cf. John 1:4,5; Colossians 1:12,13).

C. Triumph of the Prince of Glory over the prince of this world (verse 31)

Conclusion: Revelation 5:5-14

[You may simply read this passage aloud as your conclusion or you may read it with whatever comments the Holy Spirit impresses upon you.]

CHAPTER **10**

Evaluate the Topical Approach

In this lesson we will compare strengths and weaknesses of the outline for a topical talk.

Recognize the Uses

Topical outlines may be used for devotional talks, for special occasion messages, or for teaching doctrines like the following:

God	Angels	Salvation
Man	Heaven	Resurrection
Sin	Holy Spirit	Last Things
Church	Scriptures	Second Coming
Person and Work of Jesus Christ		

However, it should be recognized that these doctrines are such large topics it would often be better to give a series of expository messages on each doctrine. The series then would be considered topical, but individual messages would each be based on a longer passage of Scripture. Other verses may be used to support truths brought out in the message, but the main divisions would come from the longer passage. Such a message (lesson, sermon, or Bible study) within the series would be in the expository style.

Some examples of topical sermons in the New Testament are given next:

1. Jesus' Sermon on the Mount (Matt. 5-7) shows the *Superiority of Grace over the Law*. This is indicated often by Jesus, after quoting from the Law, saying, "But I say unto you..."

2. Peter's message in Acts 2:14-40 sets the standard for early New Testament sermons to prove, with fulfilled Old Testament prophecies, that Jesus is Lord and Christ. To the Jews and proselytes, who had come to the Jewish Feast of Pentecost, such an approach was powerful and effective. It says, "about three thousand were added to their number that day" (Acts 2:41).

3. Stephen's defense in Acts 7 also proved with a summary of Hebrew history, sprinkled with fulfilled Old Testament prophecies, that Jesus whom they had crucified is indeed the Righteous One.

Each of the above sermons in the Bible developed the message by referring to various Old Testament prophecies, historical events, and quotations. They were not sermons on one short text (textual sermon) or expositions of a longer passage (expository sermon).

God gave His inspired Word in the literary style of the East. Although our thought frequently moves from past to present to future, the logic of Bible writers often deals with a *topic* rather than time. Emphasis on a topic instead of time is especially apparent in prophecies, as we see in the following example.

Isaiah, in 9:6-7, covered a broad *topic,* the coming Messiah: "For to us a child is born, to us a son is given, and the government will be on his shoulders.... He will reign on David's throne and over his kingdom...." The text gives no indication of thousands of years between Messiah's birth and His reign on David's throne. Isaiah did not speak of the crucifixion, a particular event in the life of Messiah, until chapter 53. In the sequence of time, we now know that the crucifixion happened between Messiah's birth and His coming reign, but Isaiah did not bother to tell us that fact!

Obviously, the writer dealt in these chapters with related topics, but time was not his primary concern.

Yes, even the Bible includes topical arrangements. But a word of caution is needed. We can be guilty of missing the emphasis of a passage of Scripture by using the topical method instead of the expository method if we are not very careful.

An example of the danger of teaching our own emphasis is in 1 Thessalonians 3:12–5:3. (You will better understand the need for caution if you follow in your Bible.) In the introductory verses (3:12–4:12) the Holy Spirit's clear emphasis, through the Apostle Paul, is on loving one another and living morally pure lives in the light of Christ's return. Yet, in chapters four and five the teacher often emphasizes his own view of the time sequence of coming events while entirely omitting any mention of the Holy Spirit's application. Yet, this application constitutes Paul's prayer (3:12), God's purpose (3:13, "so that…"), God's will (4:3-6), God's call (4:7), God's teaching (4:9) and Paul's admonition (4:10-12). Perhaps there would be less bitter disagreement among the Lord's servants about such glorious topics as Christ's coming again if we were careful to pay close attention to the context in which the teaching is found. To teach or preach using the *topical* method, one must be careful that each division of the outline, with its supporting verse, is true to the context.

Let's be cautious and not teach and preach our own ideas instead of what the Lord has said (see Ezekiel 22:28). There is more danger of wrong emphases with the topical method than with the expository method.

We should not miss the possibilities for using topical messages, but we must be aware of their advantages and their dangers. Let's consider the advantages first.

Be Aware of the Advantages.

Topical messages have definite advantages. Following is a list of some of them:

- A topical message is convenient; it can be suited to any occasion—a Bible study, a devotional talk, an evangelistic sermon, a prayer meeting, a missions conference, a wedding, or a funeral.

- Topical messages are good in places where groups may be without Bibles such as community events, jails, rescue missions, or senior citizens' homes. Many readers may live in areas where very few of the believers own Bibles.

- Ideas for topics are everywhere—daily newspaper, home, industry, farms, Bible, nature, human nature. The topics are endless: Birds of the Bible, Wisdom, Marriage, Divorce, Family, Sexual Purity, Repentance, Christian Character.

Jesus' parables teach deep spiritual truths from topics related to everyday life and common knowledge. We should not treat topics as mere facts of history, biography, or doctrine. Relate them to the redemptive message of the whole Bible.

Here are two examples of using topics associated with cultures and timely events:

1. If you speak to a youth group during an Olympics year, you will do well to use the theme: Winning In Life's Race. "Go for the Gold" will be an attention-getting title. During an Olympics year you can get good illustrations from the newspaper, magazine articles, newscasts on radio and TV, and the Internet. At a library you can look up Olympic records in *Guinness Book of Records* for more illustrations.

The *World Book Encyclopedia* says, "No other sports spectacle has a background so historic or so thrilling" as the Olympic Games. The article adds that they began in Olympia, Greece, "more than 2700 years ago."[13] Therefore, the biblical illustration in I Cor. 9:24-27 is probably taken directly from the

Olympics of the Apostle Paul's day, because this epistle (letter) was written to the believers in Corinth, Greece, the country that was the home of the Olympics.

Your Bible also has excellent references about applying athletic illustrations to winning life's race: Ps. 19:5; 1 Tim. 4:7-8; Heb. 12:1-4.

Preparing a topical message outline with illustrations is often the easiest method. Source materials for Bible study and for illustrations to help apply the truth are plentiful.

2. Almost anywhere one goes, he will find that people are interested in Eskimos (Innuit) and their environment. Here is an idea for a missionary teacher in the arctic to develop about birds of the Bible. However, a teacher in a warmer climate will find that it excites interest there as well.

In a tiny Eskimo (Inuit) village on the beach of the Bering Strait, the most western point on the North American Continent, the schoolchildren's interest in birds peaks in the spring. Eider ducks make their appearance in April. Geese, brants, ducks, cranes, murres, auks and auklets come from the South across the North Pacific and Bering Sea to the Arctic Coast and the Diomede Islands. After the long, dark winter, with only seal and walrus meat to eat, boys are impatient to hunt for birds and eggs in the hills and on the tundra. This is an excellent time to draw lessons from birds of the Bible.

Jesus referred to a hen gathering her chicks (Luke 13:34), and the Bible mentions eagles, sparrows, owls, hawks, sea gulls, storks, herons, cranes, pelicans, vultures and swallows (Lev. 11:13-19; Is. 40:29-31; Matt. 10:31). From such passages we may develop lessons about creation versus evolution, compassion, protection, strengthening, and provision. And from the return of the migrating waterfowl in the Arctic the teacher can easily take advantage of the Eskimo boys' attention to the fact that God is interested in the things which interest them. You can use an encyclopedia to find out about God's creative wisdom in designing various birds' feet, bills (or beaks), claws (or talons), feathers, wingspread, incubation periods for eggs, migrations and many other facts. Prepare charts and show pictures such as those to be found in *The World Book Encyclopedia*. In your concordance or your topical index of the Bible find Scripture references to study so you can relate the wonders of nature to God's Word and its application to the lives of those to whom you speak.

Beware of the Dangers!

Along with the advantages, topical messages also have very real dangers. They should be used sparingly and wisely.

False teaching:

It is a temptation to speak on a verse without taking time to understand its context. We are in danger of ignoring the setting of the verse—the book of the Bible, the people to whom it was written (Jews, Gentiles, the Church, believers, unbelievers) and the theme of the passage. If we ignore these, we can easily misinterpret a verse, giving it a meaning that the Holy Spirit did not intend. That is a serious error. Although we do not necessarily have to explain the whole context to others, we must be sure that what we say does not contradict the passage in which it is found.

"Preach the Word," said Paul (2 Tim. 4:2). Do not take a verse out of the passage to support your own idea instead of sharing God's Word faithfully. Taking a text out of context can give it a false meaning. Some quote Genesis 31:49 as a benediction, "May the Lord keep watch between you and me when we are away from each other." Although not as serious as some errors, this is using the verse falsely. The context reveals that Laban was threatening harm to Jacob if he ever returned. Dr. Chapell says it was like saying, "Cross this line and I'll cut your throat."[14] Other misinterpretations often lead to serious errors in doctrine.

Suppose you are preparing to speak on Mark 10:18, "'Why do you call me good?' Jesus answered. 'No one is good—except God alone.'" Some false teachers use that verse to presume that

Jesus denied that He was God. It is easier to go beyond what the Bible teaches with the topical method than with other methods. Beware!

Pet topics:

It is easy to prepare messages on a subject that you enjoy very much, whether it be prayer, prophecy, or some other particular theme. But God has not called us to proclaim our hobbies or pet themes to the world. He has said, "Go into all the world and preach the good news to all creation" (Mark 16:15). He has also said, "therefore go and make disciples of all nations...teaching them to obey everything I have commanded you" (Matt. 28:19-20). Paul wrote to Timothy at length, admonishing him to teach sound doctrine and to "preach the Word" (2 Tim. 4:2).

Two dangers lie in using the topical approach frequently. First, one tends to omit large portions of God's Word that aren't as appealing to the teacher or preacher. Second, the topics that are taught may not be taught in their context. Be sure to be a preacher or teacher who "correctly handles the word of truth" (2 Tim. 2:15).

If we habitually use only topical outlines, we may speak only on our favorite topics and omit much of God's Word.

A good sign to hang over a topical outline would be: "USE WITH CAUTION!"

CHAPTER 11

Outline Your Text

Main divisions of the *topical* outline are based on verses that support the topic (theme) selected from anywhere in the Bible. Main divisions of the *textual* outline all come from the same short text of one, two, or at the most three verses. Main divisions of the *expository* outline all come from one longer passage of Scripture. These are the primary differences between the topical, textual, and expository outlines of Scripture. While these basic considerations and logical organization of your thoughts are essential, you still have a great deal of freedom in preparing your outline so that it meets your personal needs in speaking.

Freedom in making your own outline

A well-balanced outline is a tool for your personal use. Its purpose is twofold: to make the speech easier for you to give, and to make the speech clearer for the listeners to follow. Although using a balanced outline greatly increases your ability to speak effectively, you do not need to become a slave to it. The following outline by Dr. T. S. Rendall illustrates this fact.

The Living Christ and His Gospel Today

Romans 1:16, 17 "I am not ashamed of the gospel, because it is the power of God for the salvation of everyone who believes: first for the Jew, then for the Gentile. For in the gospel a righteousness from God is revealed, a righteousness that is by faith from first to last, just as it is written: 'The righteous will live by faith.'"

Introduction: Romans 1:16-17 is my life text. It is many things:
   It is the testimony of Paul himself.
   It is the theme of his letter.

1. **This statement introduces my problem.**
   A. I am guilty before God.
   B. I am condemned by God.
   C. I am rebellious against God.
   D. I am helpless without God.

2. **This statement identifies the provision I can have.**
   A. The Gospel—a righteousness from God (v.17)
   B. The Power of God
   C. Salvation

3. **This statement indicates the part I have in appropriating the divine provision –"everyone who believes."**
   A. It eliminates works.
   B. It emphasizes trust.

4. **This statement invites the participation of all who hear the message.**
   A. The Lord Jesus commanded the Gospel be taken to all nations–Mk. 16:15, etc.
   B. The Apostle Paul confirmed that the Gospel is for all nations–Jew and Gentile.

Conclusion [15]

Sometimes even the best speakers feel free to depart from strict, word-for-word balance in grammar. Dr. Ted Rendall prepares perfectly balanced outlines. However, if a division heading may be clearer when changed slightly, he uses it without balancing it exactly in every detail. In the preceding textual outline, not every word or phrase of each division is balanced. The purpose is served because the first five words of each main division are balanced and the main divisions are in a logical order. Main division 1 does not need anything more; it declares the point completely. Main divisions 2, 3, and 4, however, need more words in the sentences to complete the thoughts so they can be remembered.

Work hard to make a good outline, but remember that it is your tool, not your master. Be free to be creative as the Holy Spirit leads you. Observe Pastor Rendall's freedom to fit the outline to his own need:

- Under main divisions 1, 3, and 4, subdivisions are balanced.

- Notice, however, the freedom he exercised under Main Division 2. The fact that each subdivision names something is what balances them sufficiently, although Dr. Rendall exercised freedom in using the words in a way that was most useful for him:

  A. The gospel—a righteousness from God (v.17)
  B. The power of God
  C. Salvation

(Dr. Rendall did not use another level of subdivision headings for "a righteousness from God," because it is the only qualifier of the gospel mentioned in the text. "A. The gospel" is not divided into parts, so "a righteousness from God" is an extension of the "The Gospel" and cannot be treated as a subdivision of it.)

If this explanation is too technical, be reassured that the outline is to *serve you*, not to rule you. It should help you to keep your thoughts organized. It should not put you into a verbal straight jacket that hinders communication.

TIP:
The textual outline, based on a short text, helps us to focus on a particular passage of Scripture instead of supporting our ideas with several passages, as in the topical outline.

On following pages, the textual outline by Pastor Tom Peachey is clear, easy to follow, and understand. Refer to it often as we continue to study it for several lessons.

Where Has the Joy Gone? [16]
Text: Phil. 4:4

Introduction:

The New Bible Dictionary definition–JOY: mark of Christians.

Question: Is JOY seen —in society? —in our families?
—in our church? —in our lives?

1. **JOY Commanded** vs. 4, "Rejoice in the Lord always, I will say it again, Rejoice!"

   A. *Question:* How can joy be ***commanded***?

   B. *Answer:* Joy can be commanded because joy is in the character of God as seen:

      (1) In **Nature** – that He created. Isaiah 55:12

(2) In the **Nation** – that He chose. Ps. 126

Festivals	Banquets
Crowning of kings	Sacrifices
Dedication of Temple	Weddings

(3) In **Jesus Christ** – whom He gave. John 3:16

His *Birth*   Luke 2:10
(tidings of great joy to all)

His *Triumphal Entry*   Luke 19:37-40
(joy expressed; if not, stones will cry out!)

His *Resurrection*   Matthew 28:8
(women afraid, yet filled with joy)

His *Presence*   Psalm 16:11
("in **His** presence is **fullness** of joy")

2. JOY Located: "Rejoice in the Lord."

Joy, found only *in* the Lord; spoken of by Paul as:

A. A gift   (gift of the Spirit)   Gal. 5:22
B. A paradox   (joy in sorrow)   Col. 1:24
C. Knowledge   (of others' growth in faith) Phil. 2:1-4

1 Thess. 2:19-20, "what is *our* joy...*you* are *our* joy."
2 Cor. 1:23-2:4, "work for *your* joy...all share *my* joy."

3. JOY Maintained: "Rejoice always"

A. Joy / based *in* the Lord—will not be destroyed by:

Conflict	vv. 2-3
Anxiety (fear)	vv. 5-6

B. Joy / experienced by God's grace—expressed through:

Giving—	Lord loves a cheerful giver 2 Cor. 9:7
Working—	satisfaction, happiness in work Ecc. 5:19
Worshipping—	with gladness, joyful songs Psa. 100:2
Serving—	joyfully, gladly (or serve enemies) Deut. 28:47-48

Conclusion:

-Joy / to the Christian…as sun to a flower.
-Joy / forfeited…by settling for less…like pleasure, happiness.
-Joy / found, maintained…by opening our relationship to God.

In the above outline all three main divisions are taken from the text, Philippians 4:4. Pastor Tom's very words are not found in the text, but they summarize the three ideas he wanted to emphasize from the text.

We will analyze this outline in some detail in the next several chapters. Although it is based on only one verse, it has more details than any outline we have looked at so far. With experience, each speaker will find his or her own comfort level with a longer or shorter outline. Notice, also, that where Pastor Tom used a slash

(/), you may prefer a dash (—). In some places he has left considerable space so that parts of his division line up for seeing them easily at a glance. And in the conclusion he has used dashes and series of dots to separate words and phrases in a way that would help him to remember the complete ideas and to use dramatic pauses for emphasis in the correct places as he spoke. Wherever possible, these details have been left as Pastor Tom had them in his speaking outline, so you can see that *you* also have freedom to arrange the parts as they are most comfortable for you to use.

This freedom is much like the freedom of an accomplished musician. A pianist, violinist, or trumpeter can embellish a piece of music artistically because he has first mastered the basics. Likewise, a speaker can be effective and develop his own personal style, but first he must master basic principles and forms that are presented in the first ten chapters of this book.

CHAPTER 12

Analyze the Textual Approach

(Based on the outline of Philippians 4:4 in the previous lesson.) The outlines on the next two pages are given to show the advantage of a balanced outline over an unbalanced outline. Several examples of balanced outlines are shown in contrast to an unbalanced one.

The Balanced Outline

There are several ways to organize an outline, and numerous ways you can format your outline once you have established your main divisions. However you do it, it is important to keep it balanced. Here are some other ways Pastor Peachey could have worded his main divisions and still keep it balanced.

Examples of balanced outlines, alternatives to Pastor Peachey's:

- First possibility (*questions*):
  1. Can joy be commanded?
  2. Where can true joy be found?
  3. Can we have continual joy?

- Second balanced alternative (*statements*):
  1. Paul commanded believers to rejoice.
  2. True joy can be found only in Jesus Christ.
  3. We can have true joy in all circumstances of life.

- Third balanced example (*phrases*):
  1. The command to rejoice
  2. The source of joy
  3. The possibility of constant joy

An Unbalanced Outline

In the following example we have deliberately rewritten Pastor Peachey's outline to a show a *poorly organized, unbalanced outline* in contrast to his well-balanced one:

1. What Did Paul Command Believers to Do?
2. True Joy Can Be Found Only in the Lord Jesus Christ.
3. Continual Joy in All Circumstances of Life

Although the unbalanced divisions point to Bible truths, the speaker using them would be tied to his notes, because unbalanced divisions cannot be easily remembered. He would lose eye contact. The congregation would not find the unbalanced main divisions—a mixture of a question, a sentence and a phrase—easy to follow.

TIP:
A simple motto for outlining a speech of any kind is, "KISS: Keep It Simple Saints!"

The purpose of an outline is not to encourage people to remember the outline; it is to share simply so people can understand what God's Word says and how they should respond to it. No one remembers an outline very long—even one as clear as Pastor Peachey's in Lesson Eleven. In joyful times and in times of distress, what we will remember is God's command: "Rejoice in the Lord always." It is not important for people to remember the speaker or his outline. It is important for them to remember God's Word. Get a mental picture of the basic outline form in this sample.

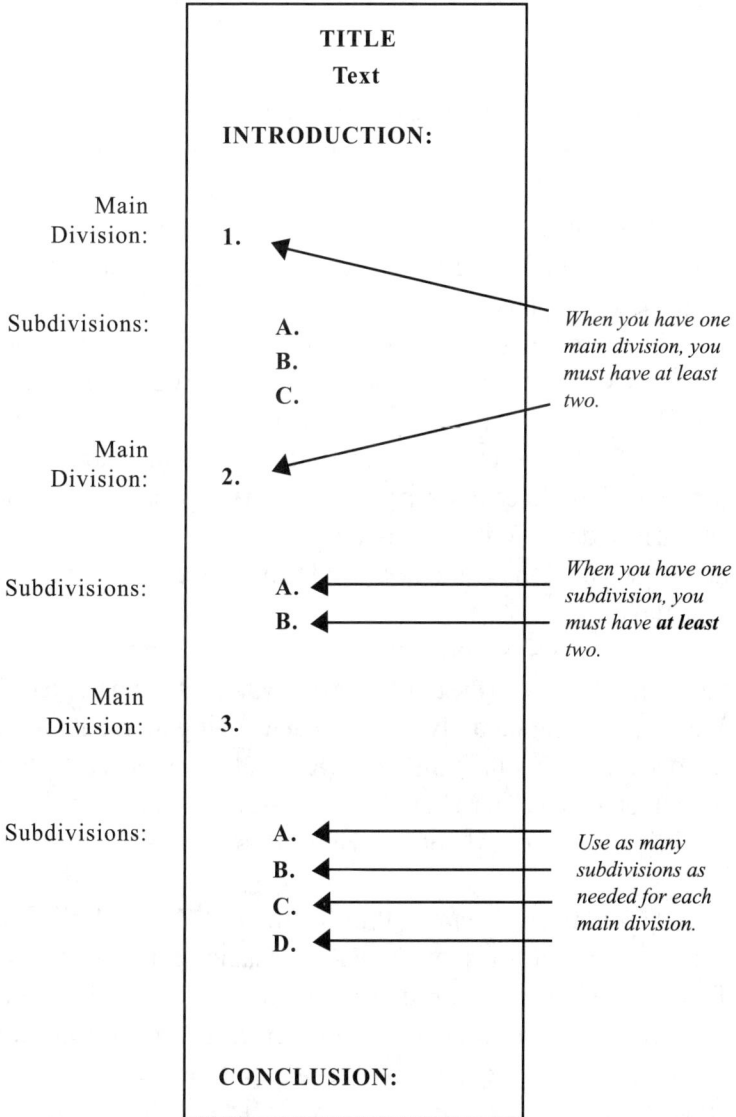

	TITLE
	Text
	INTRODUCTION:
Main Division:	**1.**
Subdivisions:	**A.** **B.** **C.** — *When you have one main division, you must have at least two.*
Main Division:	**2.**
Subdivisions:	**A.** **B.** — *When you have one subdivision, you must have **at least** two.*
Main Division:	**3.**
Subdivisions:	**A.** **B.** **C.** **D.** — *Use as many subdivisions as needed for each main division.*
	CONCLUSION:

Look at each part of Pastor Peachey's textual outline from Lesson Eleven carefully as we continue to analyze it. Although the title appears first on the page, the text is the first thing we must consider because it is the basis of the whole textual message.

The Text

Pray for guidance in choosing a text. "If any of you lacks wisdom, he should ask God, who gives generously to all without finding fault, and it will be given to him" (James 1:5).

When you are starting, choose a text that blesses *you*. That will give you confidence to share it with others and will inspire you to speak with enthusiasm.

The more you read and meditate on God's Word, the more passages will come to your mind for lessons and devotional talks. The Holy Spirit will remind you of chapters and verses. But you must put them into your mind and heart so there will be something to recall! Underline verses in your Bible that especially bless you as you read daily. Write a "T" or the word "Text" in the margin for any verse you think could be a good text for a lesson, sermon or other talk.

Philippians 4:4 is probably the best-known text on "Joy" in the Bible: "Rejoice in the Lord always. I will say it again: Rejoice!" We may not immediately see the rich teaching in it that Pastor Peachey brought out in his message. He did not see it all either until he studied it. That should make us want to study more so we can bring forth riches to others. Here are some tips:

1. *Study the context:* Philippians 4:2-7. Read all four chapters of Philippians for a better understanding. (It only takes a few minutes.) Read it through at one sitting. Then go back and read it a chapter at a time. Underline verses that speak about joy and rejoicing. For any text you must study the context. Since the subject "joy" permeates this short epistle (letter), all four chapters are appropriate as the context.

2. *As you read and study, ask the Lord to open your understanding of the text.* Learn all you can about it. When you are studying the Apostle Paul's letters (like Philippians), go back to the Book of Acts and find what Luke wrote about Paul and the church at Philippi. (Read Acts 16.)

3. *Ask the Lord to help you apply the text to your own life first.* If you are truly rejoicing in the Lord, you can speak on Phil. 4:4 joyfully! A mere explanation of the text will not necessarily bring eternal blessing to those who have come to receive God's message through you. With the Holy Spirit's working in your own life, it will bless all who hear.

4. *When you have a short text memorize it.* Even when you have a longer text such as John 1:1-14 or Psalm 1, memorize as much as you can in the time you have. Soak your mind and heart in your text.

5. *Do not expect to break down the ideas in every verse into a neat outline of three main divisions.* Like swimming or paddling a canoe, the more practice you have, the better you will be able to organize logical divisions for your outline. You may have two, three, or four main divisions. Seven should be the maximum. If you need more than seven, treat them in a series of two or more lessons.

6. *Meditate on the text.* If you can get only one thought from your text, you may need to expand the text to include another verse or two, but often meditation will reveal some other approach. Philippians 4:4 is an excellent example of a one-verse text that does not have several parts set apart as three clauses or phrases. Yet, the three-division outline derived from it is effective.

Looking at the structure of the verse, we might well ask, "What sort of sentence is this? Is it a statement of fact, a promise, an invitation or an inquiry?" No, it is a command. Main division 1. "Joy commanded," is built on the fact that it is a command.

After meditating on the verse, we would be likely to ask, "Where can I find such joy?" The prepositional phrase, "in the Lord," gives the answer, and on that thought the second main division is built: "Joy located."

As one meditates on the verse and considers the word "always," he asks how joy can be kept up; hence, the third division, "Joy maintained," is obvious.

While we meditate on a verse the Holy Spirit opens our understanding. Yet, He does not ignore our distinct personality differences. No two of us will be likely to come up with identical outline divisions.

You may teach the same verse, Philippians 4:4, with a different emphasis. Your main divisions could be as follows:

1. Rejoicing is possible in the Lord.
2. Rejoicing is possible in all circumstances.
3. Rejoicing is possible in obedience to God's command.

Another person could have these points:

1. Who is qualified to give such advice?
   [Recount Paul's extremely difficult circumstances in which he rejoiced. You will find them in the four chapters of Philippians.]
2. Why is rejoicing so prominent in the author's thoughts?
   [List the reasons for Paul's rejoicing—also given in Philippians.]
3. What is the key to rejoicing in all circumstances?
   [Develop the thought expressed in the phrase, "in the Lord."]

Asking key questions about a verse can throw light on many valuable lessons. These questions often begin with Who? What?

Where? When? Why? and How? Although not to be overdone, such questions may be used as main divisions or the answers to them may form the divisions.

7. *Usually, announce and read the text at the beginning.* That gives a basis of authority to the message. It also helps people establish the helpful habit of following in their Bibles during the lesson or sermon. However, you may sometimes read it later, as at the end of the introduction. If you are sharing with a group of teenagers at summer camp, you may get their attention better by starting right away with a story illustration that leads into the text.

CHAPTER 13

Compose the Title and Introduction

In previous chapters we have suggested that it is often better to wait until you have completed the outline before composing a title. While studying the Scriptures and organizing the ideas to develop the theme of your talk, you will often find that a good title will emerge. When some title enters your thoughts, at any time, write it down, because you may not remember it later. You may have several possible titles by the time you finish studying. Choose the one most appropriate, then modify it to make it still better if you can.

A title should attract attention as soon as someone sees or hears it. It should definitely suggest the theme of the talk in words that cause people to want to hear it. Because we are accustomed in our times to short captions for articles in newspapers, on television, on billboards beside the highway, and even on cereal boxes, people will not likely be attracted to a long title for a sermon, Bible study, or devotional talk. If you happen to pick up a book written 100 to 150 years ago, you might be amazed to read lengthy headings and titles, but not in today's books.

Titles are used mostly for church ads in newspapers, part of the order of service in Sunday bulletins, or in advertisements on radio or TV. Announcing the title before beginning your lesson or sermon is not necessary.

The introduction should capture attention immediately and lead into the message. More will be said about the introduction later in this chapter, after we discuss the title.

Understanding the Title, "WHERE HAS THE JOY GONE?"

"Joy" is a subject that interests everyone. The title of Pastor Tom Peachey's outline that we studied in chapters 11 and 12 catches attention and arouses interest. It suggests the theme, but instead of telling too much, it whets the appetite to hear more.

On the lines below, write several titles of your own for the Philippians 4:4 outline. Use a variety of styles for titles: a startling statement; an exclamation of surprise; a word or phrase that arouses curiosity, or a question. Remember that the purpose is to attract attention and create interest in the message, so think hard.

Original Statement:

_____

Original Exclamation:

_____

Original Word or Phrase:

_____

Original Question:

_____

Titles of books, speeches and sermons are sometimes dull. Perhaps authors and speakers mean for them to sound scholarly. Good titles are eye-catching phrases that attract attention. It would be difficult to get very excited over the following titles found in old books:

"The Unnaturalness of Disobedience to the Gospel"
"The General Conflagration"
"Now, Now—Not By-and-By—A Sermon to the Young"

"The Alternate Attributes"
"Christ, the Fulfillment of the Law"
"A Reply to Critics"
"Divine Teaching Gradual"
"Apostolic Exhortation"

All of these were titles of sermons by well-known preachers in the nineteenth century. The last title, above, was by the Rev. Charles H. Spurgeon, pastor of the 6000-seat Metropolitan Tabernacle in London, often called "the Prince of Preachers" and "recognized as one of the greatest preachers the world has ever known."[17] Yet, if we saw any of these titles on a bulletin board, it probably would not arouse our interest. Today, people are accustomed to more catchy titles. If the title is dull, people are not likely to come and hear the speaker. The title should not be sensational, but it should attract attention. Sensational titles may promise more than you can deliver and people will soon become unimpressed by them.

Since the title is usually the first thing a person sees or hears about a message, it is worth time and prayerful effort to make it as interesting as possible. The following titles stimulate interest:

Why Pray?	*Christmas in Prophecy*
All-Out War	*How to Know God's Will*
Secret Prayer	*The Deceiver Unmasked*
Does God Care?	*The Triumph of Calvary*
The Blessed Hope	*Whatever You Ask in My Name*
Victory—For Me?	*Under Cultivation: The*
	Attitude of Gratitude

Dr. H. A. Ironside was a master Bible teacher, author, and speaker. *Great Gospel Sermons, Vol. II*, has this to say about him, "Given up by the doctor as dead at birth, he was revived forty minutes later. As a young towhead he climbed out on a tabernacle beam and listened to Dwight L. Moody; at eighteen he was a full-fledged captain in the Salvation Army and at twenty-two he was broke, superbly confident that God would take care of him, and preaching on street corners, in missions, and in desert towns to the Indians of New Mexico and Arizona."[18] When he became the pastor of the great Moody Memorial Church in Chicago, he had no experience as a pastor.

Dr. Ironside knew the value of a title to arouse curiosity. One of his was "Fools—Wise and Otherwise." An eye-catcher, it was true to his texts, Proverbs 10:21 and 1 Corinthians 3:18.

Occasionally, words directly from a text will serve as the title. Usually, however, as in Dr. Ironside's title above, the text only suggests the title. Some titles taken directly from the words of texts are the following:

> *I Was Not Ashamed* (Romans 1:16)
> *Unsearchable Riches* (Ephesians 3:8)
> *The Precious Blood of Christ* (1 Peter 1:18-19)
> *The Alpha and The Omega, The Beginning and The End*
>   (Revelation 21:6)

A good title is relevant to the nature of the group and causes the participants to think, "That's what I need to hear."

If you are teaching a Bible class that meets regularly, such as a home Bible study on the life of Christ, or the book of Colossians, you may not need to provide an eye-catching title for each lesson. When the same classmates are meeting weekly, a title that indicates the core truth of the lesson is sufficient.

For a devotional at a weekly men's prayer breakfast, "Men's Responsibilities in the Home" may be adequate. Yet, for a breakfast meeting where unsaved men were expected, I wanted the devotional to be evangelistic and also to help born-again men see the legal basis of their salvation. I called it "A Forensic Dilemma: How Can God Be Just and Yet Justify the Guilty?" *Forensic* is often used to describe a criminal investigation. A lawyer verified my use of it for the *legal* aspect of salvation, that is, justification.

Having the title printed on a projected visual aid and on the cover of a short photocopied workbook offset the length of the title.

Be wary of trick titles. Dr. Ironside's "Fools—Wise and Otherwise," was not a trick title. It was catchy, but the text and the talk revealed that the title was right on target. We may joke about the following titles, but we should *not* use them:

"Seven Ducks in a Muddy Stream"
"Something Human Eyes Have Never Seen!"

The first one refers to Naaman dipping seven times in the River Jordan. The second one, announced widely for at least a week, had nothing at all to do with the evangelist's message. It drew a crowd. The evangelist cracked a peanut, and showed the kernels—something human eyes had never seen. Cute, but when people feel a speaker has tricked them, they lose confidence in what he has to say.

James Braga, author and Professor of Homiletics at Multnomah School of the Bible, warns: "The title should be in keeping with the dignity of the pulpit."[19] He gives the following examples of titles to avoid:

"Snoopy or Mickey Mouse"
"Wine, Women, and Song"
"An Old Testament Style Show"
"The Cats' Whiskers"
"Should a Husband Beat His Wife?"
"Smart Alec"
"Astronauts and the Man in the Moon"
"The Hot Place"
"Hippies and Mini Skirts"

Braga wisely admonishes, "Sermon headings such as these are either fantastic, coarse, crude, or irreverent, and entirely out of keeping with the sacred task of ministering the oracles of God to men." This holds true for anyone sharing the Bread of Life.

The Introduction

Purposes of the Introduction (*Introduce* means "to lead;" an *introduction* is a "lead into. "*) Following is a simple memory aid to keep in mind while preparing the introduction:

A – Attention (catch attention).
I – Interest (arouse interest).
D – Desire (create desire).[20]

TIP:

A humorous anecdote may get attention, yet leave people thinking about the story when you want to emphasize something else.

Use it only if it illustrates and leads directly into the truth you want to stress.

Don't tell a joke merely to get attention; you may quickly lose attention again.

Development of the Introduction: It is often easiest to leave the introduction until after the body of the outline is developed. By then you will have a better idea how you want to introduce your speech (lesson, sermon, devotional). However, jot down some notes whenever the thoughts come to you.

Examples of things to use in the introduction are these:

1. A poem
   - It is most effective when quoted from memory.
   - Do not quote it or read it without practice.
   - Don't read poetry in a sing-song pattern.

2. An illustration
   - Use a story, an object lesson, a recent quotation from a missionary letter, even a joke (used infrequently and with tact)—any tasteful illustration that will generate interest in your talk and lead directly into the theme or the first main division.

3. A startling statement
   - Watch folks sit up and take notice when you begin your talk by declaring, "There are more than one hundred verses in the Bible in which God says that He will *not* answer some prayers!" (Be sure you have a few references ready to defend this.)
   - Motivate people to consider what you are saying with an affirmation such as: "Only sinners can be saved and receive eternal life."

4. A thought-provoking question
   - Create a problem for your listeners to solve: "Are the heathen lost?" Then be sure your talk offers a truly biblical answer.
   - "Why do good people have to suffer?" But be careful that you do not raise a question that you cannot answer from God's Word.

CHAPTER **14**

Continue the Analysis of the Textual Outline

(Continued study based on the outline, "Where Has the Joy Gone?")

The body of the outline, consisting of main divisions and subdivisions, follows the introduction. Having captured attention in the introduction, main divisions and their subdivisions make it possible to hold the listeners' interest by arranging our thoughts in a manner that is easy to follow. Let's observe the relationship of the main divisions to the theme of the talk and to the introduction; likewise, we need to understand the relationship of the subdivisions to their main divisions.

The Main Divisions

You will usually have only three or four main divisions of an outline. They are the pillars that support the theme of the message. Each one must help to develop the theme, the central truth of the message on your heart.

Continue studying the outline, "Where Has the Joy Gone?" In Philippians 4:4, Mr. Peachey saw three main divisions, not three *parts* of the verse, but three *features*—three things that are true about the verse.

He first noticed that the whole verse is *a command*. The Apostle Paul is not saying, "Please rejoice if you feel like it." It is not a request. He does not say, "It would be so nice if you could rejoice a little more." It is not a wish. He commands the believers to *do* it. No *ifs*, *ands*, or *buts* about it. He commands us, "Rejoice." He repeats it for emphasis, "I will say it again, Rejoice!" Perhaps Pastor Tom first wrote on his paper, "Paul commanded the believers at Philippi to rejoice." He probably did not shorten it to "JOY Commanded" until later when he wanted to see it at a glance.

I was in the congregation when Tom preached and I noticed that he kept eye contact with the congregation. He was not tied to his notes by long sentences. The short main divisions were enough to help him remember the idea so that he was free of his notes. He thought on his feet and spoke spontaneously, which made me feel that he was not reading an essay, but that the message was for me.

"JOY Located," the second main division, is about the *place* where we can find real joy—"in the Lord."

The third main division, "JOY Maintained," is suggested by the fact that the text commands us to rejoice "always." The sermon told us how joy can be kept, or *maintained*, in difficult times, in circumstances we may not understand and even in times of grief.

Subdivisions of "Where Has the Joy Gone?"

Continue your personal study of the outline. Ask yourself why Mr. Peachey decided on these main divisions and subdivisions. Notice carefully how each subdivision (A, B, C) clarifies some idea of the main division.

1. **JOY Commanded**   vs. 4, "Rejoice in the Lord always, I will say it again, Rejoice!"

The first main division (above) is divided into two subdivisions (next page). Together, they indicate what the speaker wants to say about "JOY Commanded." [Using upper case (capitals) for all three letters in one word and for only the first letter in the other is merely a matter of the speaker's choice. The same applies to making some letters bold or italicized. We each develop our own little gimmicks to call our attention to expressions we want to emphasize. Underline, use asterisks, highlight words with colors, or use whatever personal helps you like in order to make it easier to emphasize certain words or phrases. It is *your* outline.]

A. *Question:* How can joy be **commanded**?

B. **Answer:** Joy can be commanded because joy is in the character of God.

Consider the two subdivisions above. Think about their relationship to the main division. *Question* and *Answer* (subdivisions) apply directly to the main division. They focus on the startling idea that joy can be commanded.

The question, "Can joy be commanded?" is challenging because it is a paradox. That is, it appears to contradict itself. As soon as you speak about joy, your hearers will think of a *feeling,* an emotion. We feel happy or sad, joyful or depressed. We might think of love, joy and peace as feelings that come and go with our circumstances. How someone treats us, whether we passed or failed a test, whether the sun is shining or rain threatens to cancel our picnic—these all affect our feelings. So, how can joy be commanded? We do not usually think of joy as obedience to a command! The hearers consider these thoughts, and the speaker suggests ideas to explain and develop the question. He guides their thoughts. Or, better yet, if you are leading a small group, ask the group whether joy can be commanded. Then ask on what basis it can be commanded according to this passage. Your outline will prompt you concerning thoughts to add to the discussion or questions to promote discussion. Consider the relationship of the subdivisions to each other.

Asking a question during a lesson causes people to think how they would answer. If you are leading a discussion, the question draws members of the group into discussion. They listen to answers in the discussion and want to know what answer God's Word will give. It is always good to keep your listeners *thinking* with you instead of your *telling* them everything.

The answer, "Joy can be commanded because joy is in the character of God," is developed by three surprising evidences of joy in God's character. They are well balanced; each is a prepositional phrase with a brief explanation:

(1) In Nature—*that He created*

(2) In the Nation—*that He chose*

(3) In Jesus Christ—*Whom He gave*

We may call points (1), (2), and (3) "*sub-subdivisions.*" These form a third level. They are the *parts* of subdivisions.

In this outline we have three *levels:*

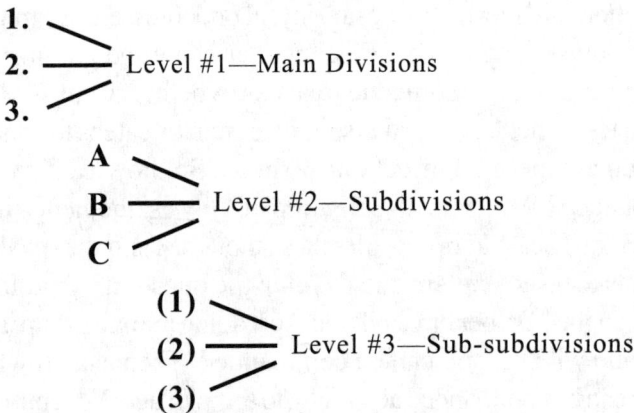

1.
2. ——— Level #1—Main Divisions
3.

   A
   B ——— Level #2—Subdivisions
   C

      (1)
      (2) ——— Level #3—Sub-subdivisions
      (3)

Any more levels would make the outline too detailed and difficult to follow. Two levels will usually be enough. If you balance the main divisions with each other and the subdivisions with each other, it is not essential to balance further brief notes that you may wish to insert in the outline from which you will be speaking.

TIP:
It is not necessary

. . .to use the very words of the text for main divisions or subdivisions.

. . .to have the same number of subdivisions for one main division as you do for another main division.

. . .to use the same style of grammar for the subdivisions under one main division as you do for the subdivisions under a different main division.

The Numbers and Letters for Main Divisions and Subdivisions

You are free to use a system of numbers and letters that will be most natural for you. Some prefer Roman numerals for main divisions, uppercase letters for subdivisions and Arabic numerals for sub-subdivisions as in the following example:

I. ——— Roman numerals: Main Divisions

A. ——— Upper case letters: Subdivisions

1.
2. ——— Arabic numerals: Sub-subdivisions

Others prefer all numerals—a mixture of Roman numerals and Arabic numerals. But you may find this more difficult to follow, because there is not enough contrast when only numerals are used.

This book uses Arabic numerals for main divisions because we use them more than Roman numerals in almost all modern numbering. Using uppercase letters for subdivisions and numbers in parentheses for sub-subdivisions provides contrast and makes it easy to glance at notes to see the next point.

1.
    A.   *Indenting each level more than*
          (1)   *the level above it makes it stand*
          (2)   *out clearly.*
    B.

2.
    A.   *Indenting also shows that*
    B.   *A and B (subdivisions) are parts of*
                         the main division above them.
          (1)   *If you have a third level, use*
          (2)   *parentheses, to avoid confusion*
          (3)   *with Arabic numerals in main divisions.*

TIP:
**You cannot *divide* something and have only one part.
You can divide it into two, three, or four parts.**

***Therefore, for divisions,* when you have a 1,
you must always have at least a 2;**

**an A must also have at least a B.
One idea may have two or more parts.**

The Conclusion

No part of your speech is more important than the conclusion. This is the final impression you will make upon your listeners. In the conclusion you apply the truth strongly. Here is where you call for a decision.

The conclusion clinches the message; it is like a hammer striking the final blow that clinches a nail. Jeremiah 23:29, "Is not my word like…a hammer…?" It leaves us with a clear understanding of what God has said in this text and the message you presented. Clinch the truth. Remember, you may do three things:

1. *Summarize the main divisions.* State each point. Do not bring in new ideas in the conclusion. If you add another illustration, be sure it is very brief.

2. *Always apply the truth you have developed.* (Sometimes you may wish to apply it without summarizing, because the Holy Spirit has clearly brought people to the point of decision.) Exhort the people to put the truth into practice.

3. *Keep it brief.* Do not ramble. Your speech is like a beautiful sweater that you have woven. Now tie the final knot. If you explain many details in the conclusion, you will run the risk of unraveling all you have done! Get right to the point. Clinch it and STOP!

You may want to summarize one message, but another time you may prefer to go directly into the final application. Either way, keep it brief.

Brief Conclusion:
summarize,
apply.

CHAPTER **15**

Recognize Strengths and Weaknesses of the Textual Outline

In this chapter we will consider ways in which the textual outline has strengths that the topical outline lacks, but we will also consider ways in which the textual outline may not be as strong for some purposes as the expository outline. The following is a textual outline:

Formula for Revival

Text: 2 Chronicles 7:14, "If my people, who are called by my name, will humble themselves and pray and seek my face and turn from their wicked ways, then will I hear from heaven and will forgive their sin and will heal their land."

Introduction:

1. "Revive" = to bring back to life or consciousness.
2. Solomon's prayer: dedication of the temple.
   Tell the story of the Temple and read aloud selections from 2 Chronicles 6:14-17, 20, 26-27, 36-39; 7:12-14.

1. God's People

A. Israel (OT: Descendants of Abraham, Isaac, Jacob)

B. Christians (NT: Born-again believers)
Matthew 8:11, "I say to you that many will come from the east and the west, and take their places at the feast with Abraham, and Isaac, and Jacob in the kingdom of heaven" (cf. Rom. 11:1-2a, 11-12, 17-18; 1 Peter 2:9).

2. God's Promise
A. "Hear from heaven"
B. "Forgive their sin"
C. "Heal their land"

3. God's Conditions
A. "Humble themselves."
B. "Pray."
C. "Seek my face."
D. "Turn from their wicked ways."

Conclusion:

[A call to Christians to meet God's four conditions and receive His threefold promise.]

In the preceding outline, both main divisions and subdivisions come from the one-verse text. This would still be considered a textual outline even if only the main divisions were from the verse. In this text it is easy to use the very words of the text for most of the subdivisions. For most texts, you must use your own words to summarize ideas.

Did you notice something unusual about this outline? "God's Promise" comes last in the verse but before "God's Conditions" in the outline. This is permissible for effect. By holding forth the promise first, the speaker causes his audience to ask themselves, "What must I do to obtain this wonderful promise?" By placing "God's Conditions" last, he answers their question. Either is a logical order.

Thank the Lord, there are honest salespeople. A Christian

salesman soon becomes known as one people can trust. A good salesman will show his customer the quality of the product he is selling and indicate to the customer his need for it. When the customer is aware of the fine quality of the product and of need, the salesman will help him arrange a plan whereby he can afford it. He will consider what payments the customer can make within his budget. If the salesman talks too soon about the cost, the customer may think, "The price is too high; I can not afford it."

Understanding that his listeners might balk at the cost of following the Lord, the speaker may present God's glorious promise first and then the very reasonable conditions He places on it. In that case, the preceding outline of 2 Chronicles 7:14 would be appropriate. However, you may prefer to present the three main divisions in the order that they appear in the verse as in the following outline:

1. **God's People**
2. **God's Conditions**
3. **God's Promise**

Another order could be as follows:

1. **What Is God's Promise?**
   Answer: It has three parts.

2. **What Are God's Conditions?**
   Answer: There are four conditions.

3. **Who Is Qualified?**
   Answer: God's people.

Although we used the textual method to illustrate how to make an outline, the same steps apply to any type of outline. What we said about the theme, title, text, introduction, body, and conclusion is good for any outline.

Strengths and Weaknesses of the Textual Method

Limiting the text to a verse or two, the speaker is not so liable to be tempted to defend his own ideas as with the topical method. However, the speaker might be tempted to speak only on texts that support the themes he likes and neglect other themes. A devotional speaker who speaks to a group occasionally or only once will find the textual method effective. On the other hand, for regular ministry to a congregation, class, or Bible study group, the expository method is best for greater depth of Bible knowledge.

Evangelists, speakers at youth rallies, and guest speakers for banquets or other special occasions often use a textual message. Time limits and the fact that people may not have Bibles to follow a longer text often make the expository method less practical.

The major concern with the textual outline is to treat the text in a manner consistent with its context. You may or may not use the context in speaking, but you must always study it so you can use the text honestly—in keeping with both the immediate context and the general teaching of Scripture. Take the following text for an example: Exodus 14:13, 14, "Moses answered the people, 'Do not be afraid, Stand firm and you will see the deliverance the Lord will bring you today. The Egyptians you see today you will never see again. The Lord will fight for you; you need only be still.'"

To use the text honestly, in keeping with the context, does not mean that you must limit your talk to the historical facts of Moses' day. Give the gist of what Moses said to the Israelites and apply the same truth to situations people face today. One way to handle this text would be to tell in your own words the story of the Israelites' crossing the Red Sea on dry ground and the Egyptians drowning (Ex. 14). That is *interpreting* the passage. Then encourage people to wait on the Lord instead of rushing ahead in the strength of the flesh. That is *applying* the truth.

While telling a story, you can read the more dramatic parts, such as Exodus 14:10-14, with feeling. I doubt whether anyone could choose more emotional words than the ones in the Bible. Use voice inflection to suggest the terror in verses 10 and 11, the sarcasm in verse 11, the bitter, rebellious anger in verse 12. Suggest the feeling; do not overdo it to the point of being melodramatic. Then, from your text (verses 13 and 14), draw out timeless principles for your main divisions. Develop these principles from the historical context, but apply them as follows to the very real problems people face today:

When you feel helpless before the enemy…

A. "Do not be afraid."
B. "Stand firm."
C. "The Lord will fight for you."

Following are some themes and texts to consider (you decide on interest-grabbing titles):

CHRISTIAN LIFE
Faith—Hebrews 11:1
Worship—Psalm 96:9
Perfect Peace—Isaiah 26:3
An Open Door—Revelation 3:8
Access to Grace—Romans 5:2
Abundant Life—John 10:10
On the Alert!—1 Peter 5:8, 9
A Broken Heart—Psalm 51:17
Prayer for Purity—Psalm 51:10
Unlimited Power—Ephesians 3:20
Grace that Works—2 Corinthians 9:8
All Our Needs—Philemon 4:19
Pruning for Fruit—John 15:2
The Tongue—James 3:5b-6
Submit and Resist—James 4:7
Learn From the Ants—Proverbs 6:6
Our God: Our Guide—Psalm 48:14

Into God's Presence—Psalm 24:3,4
A Refuge & Strength—Psalm 46:1
Revival Requirements—2 Chronicles 7:14

CHRISTMAS TEXTS
Birth of the Savior—Matthew 1:21
Christ is Lord—Luke 2:11
Two Appearings—Isaiah 9:6-7
The Virgin Birth—Matthew 1:22-23; Isaiah 7:14

MISSIONS
Universal Love—John 3:16
All the World—Mark 16:15
Power for Service—Acts 1:8
Among the Nations—Psalm 96:3
The Triumph of Missions—Revelation 7:9
The Unevangelized—Romans 15:20-21
Prayer for Revival—2 Chronicles 7:14

NATIONAL NEEDS
National Righteousness—Isaiah 26:2
Great Commission—Matthew 28:18-20

PERSON AND WORK OF CHRIST
Son of God—John 10:36
Bread of Life—John 6:35
Lamb of God—John 1:29
Eternal I AM—John 8:58
Gate (or Door)—John 10:7
In the Beginning—John 1:1
Incarnate Word—John 1:14
Way, Truth, Life—John 14:6
Good Shepherd—John 10:14
Light of the World—John 9:5

Lord and Master—John 13:13
Resurrection & Life—John 11:25

PRAYER
Approaching God—Ephesians 3:12
Purpose of Prayer—John 14:13; 17:1
Ask, Seek, Knock—Matthew 7:7-8
Priesthood of Believers—1 Peter 2:5, 9
The Way Into the Holiest—Hebrews 10:19, 20

RETURN OF CHRIST
Jesus' Promise—John 14:2, 3
The Blessed Hope—1 Timothy 2:11-15
The Purifying Hope—1 John 3:2, 3
Christ's Final Promise—Revelation 22:7, 12, 20
Living in the Light of the Coming of the Lord—
    1 Thessalonians 3:12-5:24

SALVATION, ASSURANCE
Lifted Up—John 12:32
Way to God—John 14:6
Assurance—1 John 5:13
Sons of God—John 1:12
Nice Clothes!—Isaiah 61:10
Leopard Spots—Jeremiah 13:23
Wages or Gift?—Romans 6:23
God's Personal Love—John 3:16
Lake of Fire—Revelation 20:14, 15
Christ Crucified—1 Corinthians 1:23
The Lamb of God—John 1:29
Heavenly Purchases—Revelation 3:18
Sinners One & All—Romans 3:23
Final Invitation—Revelation 22:17
Shut Out—Matthew 5:20; Revelation 21:27

How To Be Saved—Romans 10:9, 10
Message of the Cross—1 Corinthians 1:18
Price of Salvation—1 Peter 1:18, 19

CHAPTER 16

Explain, Illustrate, and Apply God's Word

"Expository" means uncovering, explaining, making something clear. An expository message explains one longer passage.

The Value of Exposition

Exposition is the best method to build people up in the faith and in their knowledge of God's Word, especially for any group that meets regularly, because it holds the speaker more closely to the Bible. It declares and explains what Scripture says and encourages people to think about it and apply it to their lives. We may enhance exposition with evidences, explanations, authoritative quotations, and illustrations. However we set forth the truth—by lecture, question-and-answer, or discussion—we draw all main-division and subdivision ideas of the expository outline from the passage of Scripture.

Amazingly, the same Scripture often builds up the Christian while convicting the unsaved and challenging the antagonist to consider what God says.

- Children's workers use exposition to teach Bible stories.
- Youth leaders lead discussions of doctrinal portions to guide teens to apply God's truth to evangelism, Christian living, and service at home and abroad.
- The adult-class teacher takes students still deeper by helping them discover life-changing truth through

studies of Bible books. They discuss practical applications to the home, the university, the work place, and are encouraged to be involved in the church's ministries (1 Thess. 4:18; 5:11).

- The pastor will devote himself to expository preaching throughout the Bible. He adapts the expository outline to book studies, biographies (stories of Bible characters), doctrines and Christian ethics in personal and civic life.

God's Word is a well that never runs dry. No matter how many times we pour out life-giving water for others, more is there for our own thirst and cleansing. New insights into truth await us at every age and in every circumstance.

Denis Lane, former Overseas Director of Overseas Missionary Fellowship, asks pertinent questions:

How many Christians really know what their faith is about? How many can give a reason for their beliefs? How many see Christian truth as a whole and where individual truths fit into the picture?...Why do our people starve in the midst of plenty? I firmly believe that it is because too often we indulge in 'blessed thoughts' and too infrequently teach the Word of God in all its fullness. We take our thoughts and hang them onto Scripture instead of allowing the Scriptures to control our thoughts. We use the text as a kind of launching platform to be left behind after take-off and never return to it.... Sincere exhortation and a fund of good stories, however, are no substitute for the convincing power and authority of the Word of God.... A simple test will show us whether our preaching and teaching are expository or not. Do our hearers feel compelled to open their Bibles and do they refer to them when we are speaking?[21]

Lane presents good arguments for planning exposition of the Scriptures so "the whole of God's plan can be unfolded" and we can deal with "important matters of Christian living in a natural way." He suggests that people will feel a greater need in their lives for their Bibles, and "ethics...will begin to take their place in the regular teaching."[22]

Recent surveys reveal that a large percentage of churchgoers cannot name the four Gospels—evidence of the need for more thorough Bible teaching.

Explain the clear meaning of a Scripture passage *in its context.* Saturate your mind and heart in the Word itself; then use whatever Bible study helps are available—a concordance, a Bible dictionary, a commentary, a Sunday School teacher's manual, or a Bible atlas. Check with your Christian bookstore or the Internet for publications to meet your particular need.

More About Interpretation and Application

It is dangerous to approach the Scriptures asking, "What does this say to *me?*" The danger is focusing on self rather than the objective Word of God. We must first ask, "What does God's Word say? What truth does it declare?"

Faith is based on fact, not how a verse makes one feel. We need to approach the Scriptures with the prayer, "Lord, give me wisdom to understand what *You* are saying," not, "Help me find inspiration for the day" (or comfort or peace or whatever makes us *feel* good). Come to God's Word with an open mind and heart to receive what He wants to teach, not searching for what we hope to find. Coming to God's Word for what it says to *me* puts me in charge, not God. Studying it with a receptive heart to find what *God* wants to say is not the same.

The Bible is inspired. Every word, although written by men, is what God wanted written. He kept all parts equally from error, so that it is truly God's own message to mankind. He protected it from all contradiction. "Above all, you must understand that no prophecy of Scripture...had its origin in the will of man, but men spoke from God as they were carried along by the Holy Spirit." (2 Peter 1:20, 21).

To state that the Bible is inspired is not to say that God dictated it all. He used the cultures, vocabularies, experiences, abilities, and personalities of the human authors. The miracle of inspiration is that men did not function as mere secretaries, robots, or tape recorders. The Holy Spirit worked with them, in them, and through them as they wrote. Therefore, David wrote in a different style from Isaiah. We can also expect different wording of the same incident by writers of the Gospels. To study diligently to find out what God was saying through the human writer to his readers at that time is what is meant by properly interpreting the Scriptures. Ask the One who inspired it to illuminate it (turn on the light).

When we have clearly established the objective truth, we can then ask, "How does this truth apply to my life today?" It may encourage, comfort, or motivate to service. On the other hand, it might convict of sin, negligence, slothfulness, lovelessness, self-centeredness—matters less stimulating than we would have desired, but what He is saying to us! We are so often telling God what we want that we don't leave Him space to get a word in edgewise.

A mission's field superintendent felt that he must send a certain new missionary home because he did not adapt to the culture and made himself offensive to other missionaries and to nationals. The superintendent prayed daily that the Lord would show him what to write on the failing missionary's report, because it was a serious step to take. Instead, from His Word, the Holy Spirit convicted him that he was not praying according to God's will. When he confessed that he had sought guidance for doing the logical thing instead of truly seeking God's will and wisdom (James 1:5), he began praying that God would bless the man and make him a successful missionary. God answered. The missionary became an effective witness for Christ, one whom everyone loved; he established more churches in that nation than anyone else in his mission. Instead of what he first asked for, the superintendent received what God wanted to give him.

Do you see the difference between approaching God's Word to find and support what you want and being open to what God is saying? *Do not place subjective, personal application* before *historical, objective interpretation.* People's ideas of what Scripture means often contradict each other. Truth never does; God's Word never contradicts itself. Therefore, we must study Scripture in its context. Application must always follow careful interpretation.

Illustrating God's Word

For a large, sophisticated congregation, a pastor used simple object lessons to hold everyone's interest in his sermon on law and grace. When he illustrated the purpose of the law as a plumb line, he dangled a weight at the end of a string. People of all ages are attracted to a visual aid, no matter how simple.

He then told about the problem he had experienced with his furnace. He held up and turned on a large flashlight and explained how he had used it to search for the trouble. Although the flashlight could expose the unlit pilot light, it could not ignite it. Likewise, God's law reveals sin, but it cannot give life. It can show us our need of God's grace, but it cannot give grace.

A missionary spoke of the many kinds of people, gifts, talents, training and methods the Lord uses to communicate the gospel. He lit a large white candle to illustrate Jesus' declaration, "I am the light of the world" (John 9:5). Several people of various ages, lit small candles of different sizes and shapes from the white candle to illustrate the source of the light. To illustrate Jesus' statement, "You are the light of the world" (Matt. 5:14), the speaker sent the people holding small candles to light candles held by folks in various parts of the congregation

Visual illustrations (objects and actions that can be seen), although simple, hold attention. Jesus used such object lessons— a coin, a fishnet, the widow's mite, a fig tree—everyday things. They are good illustrations because they are familiar and because seeing holds our attention and helps us to retain what is taught better than merely hearing. Carry a pocket-size tablet to collect ideas and write notes about illustrations you can use. Use them with all age groups.

Stories, such as Jesus' parables, are some of the best illustrations. The Master Teacher told stories about birds, a farmer, foxes, builders, wide and narrow gates, the tiny mustard seed, wheat and weeds, treasure hidden in a field, a costly pearl, yeast, sheep, vineyard keepers and tenants. You and I have Jesus' authority to teach His Word as He taught it (Matt. 28:18-20).

An illustration is a window that allows light to shine on a truth. Illustrations from books are seldom as fresh and fitting as the ones discovered in nature, science, the news, family activities, sports events, and personal experience. Illustrations are everywhere when we learn to recognize them. The more we live in the Word, the more we say of many things, "Oh, that reminds me of what I read in the Bible."

Words or phrases, such as "wise as a serpent and as harmless as a dove," will project a contrasting image across our mental screen that probably teaches more than theological definitions. Illustrative words are not limited to adjectives such as *red, brilliant, tall,* or *swift.* The nouns *mansion* and *hovel* are more descriptive than the adjectives *large* and *small* to describe living quarters. Vivid verbs—*agonize, dash,* and *terrify*—illustrate stronger feelings and more specific actions than the adjectives *worrisome, fast,* and *scary.*

Vance Havner poignantly contrasted the wisdom and wealth of Solomon to his weakness: "His career premiered in wisdom, peaked in wealth and perished with women."[23] A choice word or phrase that creates a mental picture illustrates well.

Beware of illustrating by referring to specific people, matters of personal concern, or incidents shared in private. Your knowledge about marriage problems, family troubles, and sins in the church or community must be kept in confidence. Handle news with care. Eliminate gossip! Avoid super-market tabloids. Use items only from reliable sources. Click *Delete* on many email messages.

Saving illustrations in a file cabinet, a box, or on a computer disk is wise. File them by topic or text. Use brief cross-references. For instance, with studies under James 4:7, add a note: "See illustration: *Cobra Pit*, story under C." (The story referred to illustrates "Resist the devil, and he will flee from you.") Cross reference the topic *Orphans* by adding: "See James 1:27."

Applying the Truth

God's message of grace is the Bread of Life to be shared with everyone. The goal is that each person be reconciled to God. "We are therefore Christ's ambassadors, as though God were making his appeal through us. We implore you on Christ's behalf: Be reconciled to God" (2 Corinthians 5:20-21). Therefore, we need to apply God's Word to the lives of our hearers.

We cannot stress too much that application should be made in the conclusion of the talk. Yet, application is also appropriate and often needed in other parts. You may apply truth in the introduction, the statement, and any division of the sermon or lesson. It may be a question, an exclamation, an illustration, an invitation, or an appeal.

In publicly applying Scripture to life, it is usually better to say "we" than "you." Too frequent use of *you* can sound like scolding or haranguing. Of course, it is permissible to ask the group, "Have *you* received the Lord Jesus as your Savior?" You may explain the need for a personal response, but in a public gathering do not indicate any individual. Talk to John or Mary outside the meeting, but do not address them personally in the group.

Often, people are embarrassed when called on to read or pray, because they do not read well aloud. Consequently, they may not get anything from the lesson and might not return. If unsure, ask a person earlier whether you may call on him or her to read or pray.

A gentleman confided in the author that he had experienced family problems in his boyhood that caused him always to try to melt into the crowd and not be noticed. When a teacher called on him in school, his throat constricted so that he could not speak. As an adult, he and his family visited a church, which they greatly enjoyed. After several Sundays, the Sunday school teacher called on him to lead in prayer. He was literally scared speechless! When the teacher looked up to see why he was not praying, the visitor shook his head vigorously. Finally, the teacher prayed, but the man went home that day mortified. When he returned the next week, incredibly, the same thing happened again! He never again attended that church—or any other. No one ever visited the family to encourage them to attend. He and his wife raised their children with no church influence.

Applying God's Word as we teach it is essential. Yet, it will be more effective if not overdone. As the Scripture is explained, the Holy Spirit will give ample opportunity and prompting to point out and illustrate how God wants us to respond.

Application may be a rhetorical question and, therefore, not call for response. A pastor began his introduction by asking, "Do you have joy in serving the Lord, or is it a burden and bondage for you? Are you eager to read His word and seek His guidance every morning?" By questions he opened listeners' hearts to the Spirit's application throughout the message.

As you share the Bread of Life, may God grant you wisdom (James 1:5) and bless your ministry for His glory. May He bless your public speaking with the Holy Spirit's winsome persuasion. May He enable you to claim our Lord Jesus' authority for your obedience to His commission to "make disciples of all nations" (Matthew 28:18-20).

CHAPTER 17

Include a Bridge

In your outline, to build a bridge for smooth transition from the *Introduction* into the *Body* of the outline, use the *Statement, Question*, and *Connecting Sentence.*

Statement: The speaker states in one simple sentence what he intends to explain and prove in his message.

Question: The formal label *interrogative*, often used by homiletics students, simply means *question*—a question the speaker will answer in the discourse. It is often helpful to say the question aloud, although it is not essential to do so. Repeating the question prepares people for the answer. It suggests to the listeners that everything in the body of the message contributes to answering this question.

Connecting Sentence: A simple sentence connects the introduction to the body of the message. It ties the statement and the question to the first main division. This is often called the "transitional sentence" because it connects and leads into the first main division. Each connecting sentence has a *key word* to tell us what to expect. The key word should always be plural, because it tells us what to look for in the main divisions. For instance, you may have "three *conflicts*," "five *aspects*," "seven *features*," or "four *lessons*."

To keep your outline balanced and easy to follow, do not speak of a *lesson* in one main division, a *question* in another, and a *command* in the third. One plural key word in the connecting sentence should apply to all main divisions in the outline.

Sample Connecting Sentences

For empasis, key words, always plural, are in italics in the following connecting sentences:

1. Our text has five *lessons* for the growing Christian.
2. There are three *reasons* why we should witness for Christ.
3. We see seven *opportunities* for service around us.
4. The life of Andrew shows three *examples* of a servant's heart.
5. Two *aspects* of a Christlike life invite our consideration.
6. Three *attributes* of deity call for our reverent submission to God.
7. In Psalm 23 three *relationships* between the Shepherd and His sheep assure our security and contentment in the Lord.
8. Six *evidences* demonstrate that Jesus Christ is God.

At the end of this lesson there is a list of potential key words that may be used in connecting sentences.

Sample Expository Outlines

Rev. Norman Backhouse, former Senior Pastor of Prairie Tabernacle Congregation, sometimes includes a bulletin insert with the bare outline of his sermon and with white spaces for the congregation's notes. I have included here three of his outlines from Galatians—with a Statement, Question and Connecting Sentence for each. Instead of subdivisions, the outlines add a brief interpretive statement of each main division. The first outline applies the truth throughout by adding implications for us.

The Impact of the Individual
Text: Galatians 1:1-5

Introduction: Is the Christian life just duty for you?
Are you motivated by guilt?
Do you sometimes feel trapped?

Statement: Paul's letter to the Galatian believers is the charter of Christian freedom.

Question: What areas of freedom do the opening verses reveal?

Connecting Sentence: The text reveals two areas of freedom.

1. **Our Ministry (1:1-2)**
   Paul's apostolic ministry came from the authority of the risen Lord.

   Implication: We should trust the Lord to define and direct our service for Him.

2. **Our Message (1:3-5)**
   The gospel preached by Paul was one of grace and peace.

   Implication: We should convey by our lives (in both word and deed) the true gospel of Christ's grace and peace.

Conclusion: The "Sermon in Shoes:" [With this phrase the pastor directs our attention to our thought life and plants firmly in our minds the *implications* in the main divisions.] Read through Galatians this week. Ask God to pinpoint areas of your life which need to be touched by His grace.

Pastor Norman asks three questions in the conclusion of the next outline, leading us to apply the truths to ourselves.

How Straight Is Your Walk?
Text: Galatians 2:11-16

Introduction:

[I cut the wallpaper. My wife warned me to slow down. When we had hung it, we discovered it was crooked. Now, we have a little family joke. When one hurries too much, the other says, "You might cut it crooked!"]

Statement: We need to live in "line with the truth of the gospel."

Question: What will this accomplish in the Christian life?

Connecting sentence: When we live "in line with the truth of the gospel" (2:14), we grow in three characteristics.

1. **Authenticity, not hypocrisy (2:11-13)** (Peter's behavior denies the gospel.)
2. **Courage, not fear (2:11-14)** (Paul confronts Peter.)
3. **Faith, not effort (2:15-16)** (Paul teaches justification by faith.)

Conclusion: The "Sermon in Shoes"—
Questions to ask yourself this week:

1. Where in my life can I be more real?

2. Where do I need more courage?

3. Where do I trust in myself rather than in Christ?

In the conclusion of the next outline, Pastor Norman Backhouse again applies the message with the practical phrase "The Sermon in Shoes."

Crucified for Life
Text: Galatians 2:19-21

Introduction: Sermon divisions will be interspersed with the communion service.

Statement: The Christian life is entirely by grace.

Question: In what ways does the text show that our Christian life is entirely by grace?

Connecting sentence: Galatians 2:19-21 proves the Christian life to be by grace alone in three ways.

1. **A Christian is Committed to Grace (2:19-21 and 2:15-16).**
   Christ's death ensures our acceptance before God.

2. **A Christian Lives by Grace (2:20).**
   Christ's death provides the way to life.

3. **A Christian Stands by Grace (2:21).**
   Christ's death was not in vain, it declares the God's grace.

Conclusion: "Sermon in Shoes:" Take note of your thoughts. How do they affect your relationship with God and others?

Following, a list of suggested key words may help you in writing connecting sentences.

abilities	armies	dangers
abodes	aspirations	decisions
abominations	attitudes	definitions
absolutes	attributes	deficiencies
absurdities	awakenings	demands
acceptances	beacons	devices
accessories	beliefs	differences
acclamations	benedictions	distress signals
accounts	benefits	doctrines
achievements	blessings	dwellings
acquisitions	bonds	effects
actions	boundaries	efforts
adjectives	burdens	elements
admonitions	capabilities	encounters
adornments	causes	encumbrances
advantages	characteristics	endeavors
adventures	churches	ends
affections	claims	enrichments
affirmations	commands	entitlements
ages	companions	estimates
aims	comparisons	evidences
allies	compass points	exceptions
alliances	complications	experts
allurements	components	expressions
altercations	concepts	facets
alternatives	concerns	facts
anchors	conclusions	fakes
angels	conditions	families
appearances	considerations	fears
applications	consolations	feasts
approaches	contrasts	features
approvals	criteria	festivals
arenas	crowns	fetters
arguments	currents	flowers

forces
forfeitures
foxes
freedoms
functions
furnishings
gains
giants
gifts
goals
groups
guarantees
habits
hallmarks
handicaps
harmonies
hazards
hindrances
hopes
ideals
ideas
illusions
incidents
inferences
ingredients
insights
—isms
instructions
issues
intentions
invitations
items
joys
judgments
kernels

keys
key words
kinds
laws
lessons
lies
limits
lists
losses
luminaries
lures
manifestations
marks
masks
masters
means
measures
members
messages
methods
mistakes
motives
names
necessities
needs
opinions
paradoxes
parts
people
persons
perils
points
practices
problems
proofs

propositions
qualifications
qualities
questions
reasons
recommendations
remarks
responses
routes
rules
secrets
sins
solutions
sources
statements
steps
suggestions
teachings
thoughts
topics
trials
truths
uses
verdicts
viewpoints
views
virtues
wants
warnings
words
works
worries
wrongs
yokes
youths

CHAPTER 18

Outline a Longer Passage

We have evaluated topical and textual outlines, and we need to evaluate the method that helps us to expound a longer passage of Scripture, the expository outline.

Value and Use of Exposition

Exposition, as we saw in previous lessons, builds up a congregation in the knowledge of God's Word and faith. Christians should hear expository messages week after week from the pulpit. Exposition is also best for home Bible studies, Sunday school classes, campus Bible studies, and any study groups that meet on a regular basis. Whether in evangelistic Bible studies or those for believers, the Holy Spirit blesses His Word. The expository lesson allows Him to direct our thoughts rather than tempting us to choose texts to support our pet interests. It honors God because it honors His word. Speaking directly from your open Bible also supports your words with God's authority.

That is not to say other methods have no place as we share God's Word publicly. We have mentioned that a devotional talk, an inspirational or evangelistic message, or a talk at a luncheon may call for a simple, textual address. If people do not have Bibles with them, they can concentrate on a short text and remember it better than a longer one. However, the Holy Spirit may direct us to use any method—topical, textual or expository—on any occasion.

Although exposition usually deals with a longer passage within one chapter, sometimes the context may indicate the need to include verses in the preceding chapter or the following chapter.

Use your Bible now.
The following paragraphs will be meaningful
only as you refer to each passage mentioned.

A lesson on the New Jerusalem, Revelation 21, would surely need also to incorporate at least Revelation 22:1-6. While verses from other parts of the Bible could support or further explain the divisions, all main divisions and subdivisions should be based directly on Revelation 21:1-22:6.

Likewise, a study of the Rapture can be developed from 1 Thessalonians 4:13-18. However, you may prefer to include the teaching about the Second Coming in Chapter 5:1-11. Paul, the Apostle, wrote 1 Thessalonians as a single epistle or letter, not as five separate chapters. The chapter and verse divisions were added for convenience in finding the place to read. Therefore, we should not be bound by chapter endings. Often, they will form a logical stopping place for a text, but not always.

Suppose you teach the 1 Thessalonians passage to a class of teens or adults. In your introduction, stimulate discussion with questions: "Why did God give us these prophecies? Was it merely to satisfy our curiosity about the future?" Suggest that they find a reason or reasons in the context.

When someone answers that 4:18 tells us to "comfort each other with these words," ask what other words are used for *comfort* in other versions. Some may read, "strengthen," "build up," or "edify." Someone might notice that 5:11 repeats that admonition. Commend them for their observations. Call on the group to discuss *how* they might encourage or build one another up in the light of this Scripture portion.

After the discussion about comforting or encouraging one another, suggest that they look back at the setting of the passage, the context. How does God want believers to live as they wait and look for the Rapture?

Some may realize that Paul did not just drop this prophetic treatise into his first letter to the Thessalonian believers to satisfy their curiosity about when Christ would return. Call the group's attention to 4:1-12 to learn "how to live to please God" (verse 1). Encourage them to discover 3:12-13. How often have you heard the subjects of love, sanctification, and avoidance of sexual immorality in a lesson or sermon on "The Rapture" or "The Second Coming"? Most of us must answer, "Seldom, if ever." Yet, teaching this Scripture should include them, because Paul admonishes believers about these subjects in connection with teaching about Christ's return for His Bride.

Teaching the Scriptures in context will deal with real-life, present-day needs far more effectively than isolating a topic will. The Apostle Paul's epistles (letters) each present solid doctrinal basis in the first half and practical application to Christian living in the second part.

Actually, a Sunday school teacher usually has more time to develop such an expository approach to a passage than the pastor does in his sermon. However, if it is too much for one class period, rather than rush to "finish the lesson," carry it over to the next class meeting. But plan it; don't just run out of time and the opportunity for application.

Many Sunday school classes use quarterlies from their denomination or an interdenominational Christian publisher. The quarterlies, so named because they are published four times a year, contain commentaries in magazine format on each Sunday's lesson. However, you will be freer to encourage and listen to students' questions and comments and to follow the Holy Spirit's leading in dealing with their needs if you are not bound to the thoughts in the teacher's quarterly. If you are accustomed to teaching directly from the quarterly, teaching with only your open Bible before you will take some courage, but it will drive you and your group deeper into the Word. What a blessing! It will motivate your students to study God's Word. Quarterly-oriented teachers often act as though finishing the lesson is a worthy teaching aim. It may not be. Too often, it can be a detriment to the leading of the Holy Spirit. The teacher's use of a quarterly should be restricted to preparation time like any other commentary or study help. The class whose teacher honors the Bible above any other book is blessed indeed.

With an expository outline you can guide the class through the passage—whether in one class period or more. Consider definitions of the teaching/learning process:

---

1. LEARNING IS THE DISCOVERY AND *APPLICATION* OF KNOWLEDGE.

Rote learning (parroting words) will not likely produce spiritual results, but learning by discovery and application is at a deeper level. It has been truly said, "No learning has taken place until behavior has been changed."[24] Desirable change in behavior may be conversion, growth, or change of purpose and direction. It may be a slight change or dramatic change such as the reversal of one's direction in life involved in repentance and conversion.

2. TEACHING IS
GUIDING THE LEARNER.

In addition to the statement about the relationship of learning to changed behavior, an equally true statement is, "No teaching has taken place until someone has learned." Teaching cannot be confined to *telling*. We can never be sure that anyone has learned simply because someone else has talked. The Christian teacher, therefore, might well add the next step.

3. CHRISTIAN TEACHING IS
GUIDING THE LEARNER
IN *DISCOVERING* AND *APPLYING*
GOD'S WORD
TO HIS OR HER LIFE.

When we *guide* the learner in discovering truth, we depend upon the Holy Spirit to give us wisdom and to illuminate the Scriptures to the learner. To *illuminate* is to *turn on the light*. Prayerfully guide your students so they can have the personal experience of the Holy Spirit's shining new light on Scripture. Use a quarterly only as a resource. Teach the Bible itself.

Following is another sample expository outline.

Looking for That Blessed Hope
Text: Titus 2:11-15

Introduction:
[Prayerfully consider how you will introduce the message.]

Statement: Our Blessed Hope is steadfast and sure.

Question: What is this hope like?

Connecting Sentence: We will look at three *features* of the Blessed Hope.

1. **The blessed hope involves eager expectancy** (v. 13).

   A. Definition of *hope* (example: "assured reality, yet future)
   B. Explanation of "waiting for" (NIV)
   ("Looking for" KJV)
   C. Description of "the glorious appearing"
   D. Establishment of "the blessed hope"

2. **The blessed hope is anchored in the bedrock of grace** (v. 11).

   A. In God's Person (Grace: an attribute of God)
   B. In God's Word (Grace: the message of the Bible)
   C. In Jesus' sacrifice (Grace: the essence of the gospel)

3. **The blessed hope is relevant** (meaningful) **for our lives today** (vv. 11-14).

   A. Confess Christ and believe the gospel (v. 11).
   B. Share the message before the age of grace ends (v. 11).

C. Say, "No," to ungodliness and worldly passions (v. 12).
D. Live a self-controlled, upright, godly life (v. 12).
E. Look eagerly for His appearing (v. 13).
F. Remember, you are being purified for His own (v. 14).
G. Be eager to do what is good (v. 14).

Conclusion: Let's examine our lives, then live them in the light of "the blessed hope—the glorious appearing of our great God and Savior, Jesus Christ."

Here is an expository outline for Sunday school teachers. Use it for class discussion.

The Return of Christ
Text: 1 Thessalonians 3:11-5:11

Introduction: You may introduce this lesson with a story of some personal experience—perhaps a time when someone waited a long time for you to return and thought you were not going to come, but you did return just as you had promised.

You may prefer to tell the story of King Saul in 1 Samuel 13:5-14.

Tell how the disciples thought that Jesus had come to free Israel from Rome and set up an earthly kingdom because they did not understand from the Old Testament that there would be two appearings of the Messiah.

Statement: Jesus promised in John 14:6 to come again to receive us to Himself.

Question: What lessons does the Holy Spirit teach about Christ's promised return?

Connecting Sentence: In Paul's First Epistle to the believers at Thessalonica the Holy Spirit teaches us three vital lessons about Christ's return.

1. **How to live in order to please God as we await His return** (1 Thessalonians 3:12-4:12)
   [Motivate class members with leading questions. Guide them in verse-by-verse discussion. Word your subdivisions from the things God tells us to do as we wait for Christ's coming (3:13b; 4:14).]

2. **How the Rapture of believers will take place** (4:13-18)

   A. What about believers who have died? (Discuss 4:13-16.)
   B. What about believers who are still alive? (Discuss 4:15, 17.)

3. **How the Day of the Lord will take place** (5:1-11)

   A. What is the warning for unbelievers? (Discuss 5:1-3.)
   B. How are believers encouraged? (Discuss 5:4-11.)

Conclusion: Invite members to receive Christ as Savior. We do not have to wait until someone preaches a sermon to give an invitation. Be alert to the convicting power of the Holy Spirit. The Sunday school class is a great harvest field. You may also invite believers to dedicate their lives fully to Christ.

CHAPTER 19

Be Creative

When you understand the basic distinctions between the topical outline, the textual outline and the expository outline, as taught in previous chapters, you are free to be creative. Remember, outlines are tools—good tools for public speakers, but only tools, nevertheless. Their primary function is to help you present your speech in a manner that is easy to follow. They are not rigid rules that must always be obeyed in every detail! A beginning piano student who does not obey the rules produces discord, but a concert pianist has leeway to improvise with personal style and variations.

As an example, let's study an outline about the Holy Spirit's Person and ministry from Jesus' Upper Room Discourse in John 14, 15, 16. In these chapters Jesus was preparing His disciples for the task that lay ahead after His return to the Father. A number of topics—such as asking in Jesus' name, the unity of the Godhead, the ministry of the Holy Spirit, Christ as the Vine and believers as the branches, and others—are interwoven throughout to form a beautiful tapestry. This lesson treats one topic. However, it is not strictly a topical outline. It is expository, because it takes its theme and all its divisions from one longer passage of Scripture. Yet, it is not an exposition of the three chapters, because Jesus discussed more topics in them than we are trying to cover in one lesson. We will call this a topical-expository outline.

Proper preparation will include reading through the three chapters at one sitting several times to put the verses on the Holy Spirit in perspective. Keep in mind that the suggestions for using the various parts of the following outline in a teaching situation are only suggestions. Plan well, but allow the Holy Spirit to guide you in directing the class discussion about Him.

Meet My Companion
Text: Selected portions from John 14, 15, 16

(A topical-expository outline to teach by the discussion method in teen or adult Sunday school or Bible-study groups, with portions of the text introduced throughout the lesson.)

Suggested aim: That my group members will personally invite the Holy Spirit to do His good work in their hearts.

Introduction: (Only a suggestion. Feel free to create your own Introduction.)

May I introduce my Friend and Companion who is already known to some of you? If He is not yet your constant Companion, He wants to be and can be, starting today. We know Him as the One who convicted us of sin, convinced us of our need for a Savior and wooed us to the Lord Jesus Christ. He is the One who regenerated us—made us new creatures in Christ when we trusted Him as our personal Savior. He sanctifies us, prays for us, teaches us, and has made our bodies His abode. He is our Guide, Helper, Counselor, Friend, Comforter, Encourager, and constant Companion—God the Holy Spirit.

Chapters 14, 15 and 16 of The Gospel of John contain a compact theology about the triune Godhead, prayer, prophecy, faith, and love. The Vine-and-branches passage in chapter 15 is a unique parallel with Christ and His Church. Woven throughout is the golden thread of Jesus' own teaching about the promised Holy Spirit and His ministries to the Church.

Reading the Text: (Be sure that a Bible is provided for each person. The sample announcement of the text in the next paragraph provides time for class members to find it. Notice italicized repetitions of the text. Start reading only when everyone has found the place. Provide extra Bibles of the same version you are using and announce the page number in the visitors' Bibles.)

We will study several portions of these chapters. Let's begin by reading *John 14:15-26*. Please open your Bibles to *John 14* so you can follow as I read—beginning with *verse 15*. Here, Jesus introduces His disciples to the Person whom the Father will send in Jesus' place when He returns to the Father. Follow in your Bibles as I read *John 14:15-26*. [Remember that giving the reference three times is deliberate in order to allow everyone to follow the passage as you read aloud. When you finish reading, move on to the statement, question, and connecting sentence.]

Statement: The Holy Spirit enables us to live holy lives for the glory of God.

Question: How does the Holy Spirit enable us to so live as to please to God?

Connecting sentence: the Holy Spirit will lead us along *three paths* for God's glory.

1. **First path: Obeying Jesus Christ's commands**

   A. **Obedience: the product of our love for Christ**
      (John 14:15, 21, 23a)

      (1) NOT the product of duty (law-keeping for salvation).

(2) NOT the product of chance.

(3) BUT the product of love. ("If you love me, you *will* obey," vv.15 and 23.)

B. Obedience: the product of Christ's love for us (John 15:9-12, 17)

(1) We love Him because He loved us.

(2) We love others because He loved us.

(3) We obey His command because He loved us…
  - by loving others
  - as He loved us.

C. Obedience: the evidence of discipleship (John 13:35)

(1) NOT by our church attendance.

(2) NOT by how well we defend the Bible.

(3) NOT by how much money we give.

(4) BUT by one thing—we love one another…
  - Not because the other person is lovely.
  - Not because the other person loves us.
  - But because "Jesus loves me; this I know, for the Bible tells me so."

2. Second path: Understanding the Spirit's nature

A. He is the "Paraclete." John 14:16, 26; 15:26; 16:7 (No English word includes all that this word means.) Thayer's Greek Lexicon translates it as **"advocate:"**

  (1) one who pleads another's cause before a judge…a **counsel for defense**

  (2) an **intercessor**… [see: Romans 8:26, 27]

  (3) a **helper**…**aider, assistant**; to take the place of Christ…to lead to a deeper knowledge of gospel truth and to give divine strength needed to enable [us] to undergo trials and persecutions. [Bold lettering is added for emphasis.]

Comments: We pray for the power of the Holy Spirit. Why? Power for what?

Do we want power to obey? The Holy Spirit enables us to obey Jesus' command.

B. He is "Another" John 14:16, "another comforter," a called-alongside-One like Christ. [Christ is also called "Paraclete" in 1 John 2:1 ("Advocate," KJV; NASB; "One who speaks to the Father in our defense," NIV; "One who pleads our case," WILLIAMS.)]

C. He is a Faithful Companion John 14:16, "with you forever."

Illustration: MYSTERY—Jesus, "I am with you always, to the end of the age" (Matt. 28:20). **BUT** also, **"I am going ... I will come back"** (John 14:1-3).

Problem: How can both be true? (Matt. 28:20; Jn. 14:1, 2)

Answer: John 14:16-17, 18-20; the Spirit of Christ comes to live in us. Therefore, Jesus, who is physically at the Father's right hand as the resurrected Son of Man, is also spiritually with us. In fact, He dwells **in** us.

D. He is the Spirit of Truth (John 14:17).

Illustration: We can not trust credit cards, presidents, prime ministers, royalty, the economy, or politicians. We can not always trust Christians. We can't even trust ourselves! The value of money changes daily. Perceptions of time and space are relative. But there is absolute and eternal TRUTH.

(1) (14:6) Jesus: "I am...**the truth**...."

(2) (14:16) "Another Paraclete" ...not another truth, but the Spirit of Christ, who is **THE TRUTH**;

(3) (15:26) "...the Spirit of (the) **truth**...will testify about me."

(4) (16:13) "He will guide you into all (the) **truth**."

Illustration: Pilate, "What is truth?"
Humanists, relativists ask: "What is truth?"
Jesus declared: I am the truth."

E. He is the Holy Spirit (John 14:26).
   (1) "Spirit"
      a. Jesus in the flesh: one place at a time.
      b. Spirit permeates material, physical and spiritual.
      c. *Therefore*, Jesus said, "It is for your good that I am going away. Unless I go away the Counselor (Paraclete) will not come to you," (16:7).

   (2) "Holy," also: "Spirit of Holiness"
   Consider some of His names:

Holy Spirit	Spirit of Grace
Spirit of Burning	Spirit of Life
Spirit of Truth	Spirit of Glory
Spirit of Promise	
Spirit of God and of Christ	
Spirit of Wisdom and Knowledge	

3. Third Path: Understanding the Spirit's ministry

A. Personal ministry (14:17-18)
(1) "**He** lives *with* you"
(2) "and will be *in* you...."
(3) "I will come to you."
  - True of Jesus' personal return (14:1-3).
  - Yet, in this immediate context, seems to pertain to Jesus' coming in the Person of His Holy Spirit to indwell believers.

B. Teaching Ministry
(1) Personal Tutor in Jesus' teachings (14:26)
(2) Our own Guide into truth (16:13; cf. 14:6)
(3) Never contrary to God's Word (Bible) (16:13b)
(4) Prophetic (16:13c)

C. Convicting (convincing) Ministry (16:7-11)—convicting of guilt in regard to:
(1) Sin—"because men do not believe in me (Christ),"
(2) Righteousness—"because I (Jesus) am going to the Father," (the Holy Spirit would, therefore, be the One to bring this conviction)
(3) Judgment—"because the prince of this world now stands condemned."

D. Glorifying Ministry
(1) Testifying about Jesus Christ (15:26-27)
(2) Glorifying Jesus Christ (16:14)

Conclusion:

> Come, Holy Spirit, heavenly Dove,
> With all Thy quickening powers;
> Kindle a flame of sacred love,
> In these cold hearts of ours.
> Come, shed abroad a Savior's love,
> And that shall kindle ours. (Isaac Watts)[25]

The suggested Statement, Question and Connecting Sentence prepare the class for the line of thought in the Body of the outline. Notice the key word *paths*. When the lesson is set forth so students know exactly what to expect, it is easy for them to learn. In this lesson they are looking for three paths by which the Holy Spirit leads us to live holy lives for God's glory. We will give teaching suggestions for the first main division with its subdivisions. You may develop your own plan for teaching the other two main divisions with their subdivisions. You may also want to add more thoughts to the teaching about the Holy Spirit, and much more about the other great truths that form the threads of this rich tapestry (John 14-16 or John 13-17).

Suggestions for Teaching 1, A by Discussion

1. **First path: Obeying Jesus Christ's commands**

   A. **Obedience: the product of our love for Christ**
      (John 14:15, 21, 23a)
      (1) NOT the product of duty. (Law-keeping for salvation)
      (2) NOT the product of chance. (Not: "Please consider obeying Me!")
      (3) BUT the product of love. ("If you love me, you will obey.")

Read John 14:15-23 aloud, ask for a volunteer to read it, or call on someone. However, be careful. Reading aloud is painful for some people. Do not call on a visitor, only someone whom you know to be comfortable with reading aloud to a group—and someone who projects the voice and enunciates clearly. If a Sunday school class has the misfortune to sit in straight, immovable pews, folks in the back rows will not hear a person reading in the front row. It is very difficult to hear a person who is facing away from you! Those with hearing impairment (including most older people) need our consideration.

Turn the first main division into a question. Ask, "What path is revealed in verses 15, 21, and 23?" If necessary, supplement with another question, "How can we live to please God?" Depending on the translations in use, one may answer, "Keeping Christ's commandments," or another, "Obeying Christ's commandments."

Ask, "What do these three verses (15, 21, and 23) say will produce such obedience to Christ?" Then follow up with questions of your own to lead them to the conclusions in subdivisions (1), (2), and (3).

Instead of suggesting, "Obeying Jesus Christ's commandments," as the path revealed in these verses, someone may well suggest, "The path of love for Jesus." Do not try to compel your group members to come up with same wording you have in your outline. Listen for acceptable ideas. Commend them for their insight and adapt your next question accordingly: "What will love for Jesus produce in us?" Remember that your outline is to guide you, not to enslave you. Be versatile.

Encourage questions and opinions from the group. Do not be afraid that discussion will lead you away from your prepared outline; never let the outline or the quarterly become your master instead of your servant! The Holy Spirit will guide you and help you to think in a leader's role instead of merely a lecturer's role.

If comments lead too far from the subject of the passage, repeat the question used earlier: "How does the Holy Spirit enable us to live in a way that is pleasing to God?" Then call on someone else: "Susan, do you see a difference between this path of obedience and the notion that a person must obey the Ten Commandments to be saved?"

Suggestions for Teaching 1, B by Discussion

B. Obedience: the product of Christ's love for us
(John 15:9-12, 17)
   (1) We love Him because He loved us.
   (2) We love others because He loved us.
   (3) We obey His command because He loved us...
   • by loving others
   • as He loved us.

Ask the group to look for further teaching concerning obedience and love in John 15:9-12, 17. Continue encouraging them to find truth that will help them to live so as to please God. Cultivate an atmosphere in which they will feel free to ask questions or even to see something differently from the way someone else sees it. God's Word says, "As iron sharpens iron, so one man sharpens another" (Proverbs 27:17). Such interaction causes us to think and to search the Scriptures; it gives us a chance to receive the Holy Spirit's illumination of His Word to us. Involvement will produce far deeper understanding than merely accepting something because "the teacher said so." It will also motivate members to study the Bible lesson before coming to class.

This is not the question-and-answer method, but you need to have questions prepared to use when needed to move the discussion along in the right direction. Instead of declaring each subdivision as a statement, ask questions such as the following:

   • What prompts our love for Christ?
   • How is that love evident?
   • Why would we love others, even if they are unlovely?
   • What motivates obedience to Christ's command?

- How is our obedience to Christ's command demonstrated?
- To what extent are we to love others?

Have a few written questions to refer to, but use only the ones you need to draw the members into discussion. When a person answers, follow up with another question—to the one who answered, to another person, or to the group in general. Ask, "Which verse supports this?" Or, ask, "How does Jesus' teaching compare or contrast with our natural inclination?" Be prepared to share Isaiah 55:8 if someone else does not.

You must stay alert, listening to what your group members say, so you can encourage discussion and application by comments, questions and directing them to verses of Scripture. Keep in mind that your preparation and use of questions and comments are not to tell what you have learned, but to guide in the discovery of truth in a way that the Holy Spirit can use His Word to teach in a deeper and more permanent way than you can.

Suggestions for Teaching 1, C by Discussion

C. Obedience: the evidence of discipleship
   (John 13:35)
   (1) NOT by our church attendance.
   (2) NOT by how well we argue about the Bible.
   (3) NOT by how much money we give.
   (4) BUT by one thing—we love one another...
      - Not because the other person is lovely.
      - Not because the other person loves us.
      - But because "Jesus loves me; this I know, for the Bible tells me so."

From time to time, have other verses ready to ask a volunteer to read, or read it yourself, for enrichment of the group's ideas.

Encourage students to share verses and experiences that illustrate what you are studying.

Have in mind simple diagrams to write on a chalkboard illustrating meaningful truths your students point out. Confirming their ideas in this way is a reward that encourages learning far more than your finding the truth and telling it to them. You are guiding the learner in his own discovery of truth.

Following are some verses and a diagram that can be used in this lesson:

He "loved me and gave himself for me" (Gal. 2:20).

"But God demonstrated his own love for us in this: While we were still sinners, Christ died for us" (Rom. 5:8).

"God has poured out His love into our hearts by the Holy Spirit, whom he has given us" (Rom. 5:5).

"My command is this: Love each other as I have loved you" (John 15:12).

Illustration:

You may draw this illustration on a chalk board, overhead transparency, or poster.

VERTICAL

Jesus' love for us.

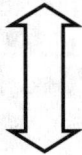

↕

Our love for Him.

HORIZONTAL

Our love for others.

"We know that we have passed from death to life, because we love our brothers. Anyone who does not love remains in death…. This is how we know what love is: Jesus laid down his life for us. And we ought to lay down our lives for our brothers" (1 John 3:23).

A triangle illustrates the flow of **God's love in Christ:**
1. God loves me.
2. I love others.
3. Others respond to God's love through me.

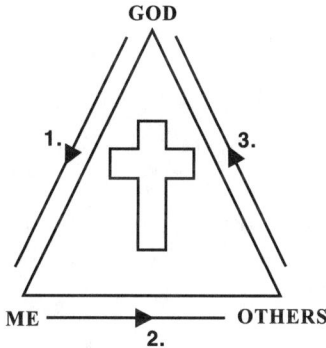

Continue preparing the second and third divisions of your lesson with their subdivisions for guided discussion. Be an active member of the group, but remember that as the leader of the discussion you have the responsibility:

(1) to encourage participation,
(2) to prevent anyone (including yourself) from monopolizing the discussion, and
(3) to keep the discussion on the subject.

You will be surprised how fast the time goes, and you may

decide to continue the lesson for several class periods. Active involvement that produces heart-searching, encouragement, conviction, repentance, spiritual growth and dedication is more important than covering all the material.

The expository outline allows for variety. It may be developed from a few (three to five) verses, a longer passage, several chapters, or even from a special topic within one longer portion. You may prefer to teach Jesus' Upper Room Discourse in the order of the chapters and verses.

CHAPTER **20**

Put It All Together

Sharing the Bread of Life is the work of the Holy Spirit, who indwells and empowers believers to be witnesses for Christ.

The Holy Spirit revealed His Word to prophets of old; He also inspired what they wrote in the Bible so it accurately and fully recorded the Word of the living God without any contradiction or error. "And we have the word of the prophets made more certain, and you do well to pay attention to it, as to a light shining in a dark place, until the day dawns and the morning star rises in your hearts. Above all, you must understand that no prophecy of Scripture came about by the prophet's own interpretation. For prophecy never had its origin in the will of man, but men spoke from God as they were carried along by the Holy Spirit" (2 Peter 1:19-21).

The Holy Spirit illuminates His Word to the hearts and minds of believers today, giving them spiritual understanding and wisdom. "The unfolding of your words gives light; it gives understanding to the simple" (Psalm 119:130).

The Apostle Paul prayed that believers might "be filled with the knowledge of [God's] will through all spiritual wisdom and understanding" (Colossians 1:9). Through James, the Lord promised wisdom to anyone who requests it if he asks without doubting (cf. James 1:5,6).

The *number one priority* in preparation for sharing the Bread of Life is to *ask God for wisdom*. Teaching, preaching, giving a devotional talk, leading a Bible study—these are not mastered from exercises in a book or a class in public speaking. Techniques for public speaking can be learned from secular books by teachers such as Dale Carnegie. But persuasive, spiritually convicting power is given by the Holy Spirit. Therefore, begin your preparation for every talk, lesson, or sermon in diligent prayer. We have Jesus' own promise, "Ask and it will be given to you; seek and you will find; knock and the door will be opened to you. For everyone who asks receives; he who seeks finds; and to him who knocks, the door will be opened" (Matthew 7:7,8).

Studying God's Word

Saturate your mind with the Word of God. Academic knowledge of the Bible (a head full of information, knowledge of facts) is not enough. "Do your best to present yourself to God as one approved, a workman who does not need to be ashamed and who correctly handles the word of truth" (2 Timothy 2:15). This involves more than just studying the week's lesson. "Your statutes are my heritage forever; they are the joy of my heart" (Psalm 119:111).

Plan #1: Read the Entire Bible According to a Plan.

Why not? We read a biography, novel or textbook completely. Establish the daily habit of reading the Bible devotionally. Devotional guides can be a blessing, but they can also be a severe hindrance if we limit our Bible reading to them. Let them be supplementary, not our primary source of devotional reading. Hymns and Christian biographies, books on Bible doctrines and worship, missionary periodicals, and many other materials can enrich our devotional reading. However, nothing can take the place of simply reading the Word of God daily. The One-Year Bible, published by Tyndale House, has the entire Bible arranged in 365 daily readings. It averages about three to four pages of the Bible daily. We can read that many pages at one sitting or half in the morning and half at night. Action International Ministries offers Doug Nichols' small yearly Bible-reading schedule that you can carry in your Bible. But whatever plan we use, we need to read the Bible through regularly.

Plan #2: Study Books of the Bible.
We can benefit by concentrating on one book of the Bible or one portion of a longer book—reading and re-reading daily until it is very familiar. We can easily read a New Testament epistle at one sitting, such as any of Paul's shorter letters, James', Peter's, or John's epistles. The average reading time for such a short New Testament book is about fifteen minutes. Several take less time. Longer ones like Romans or Hebrews, with thirteen to sixteen chapters, may be read in three or four sittings, whatever you are comfortable with. We can mentally digest longer books such as Genesis (fifty chapters), Isaiah (sixty-six chapters), or Matthew (twenty-eight chapters) by reading a logical section like the Creation account, the Joseph story, or several chapters of Psalms at one sitting.

Reading a short book like Colossians at one sitting (fourteen or fifteen minutes) at least once a day for two weeks, will provide us with an appreciation and knowledge of the book that we will never lose.

Such knowledge contributes immeasurably to good Bible teaching. Daily Bible reading develops a wealth of knowledge for the Holy Spirit to draw from. Merely studying the lesson in a quarterly or manual can not produce the kind of Bible teacher that faithful reading of God's Word can. No amount of formal Bible training, as valuable as it is, can take the place of fervent Bible reading. The Book of Revelation promises blessing to the person who reads it (Rev. 1:3).

Vance Havner, beloved Southern Baptist evangelist and author, told the story of "the old bootblack in the barbershop" who always had his Bible close by. One day a customer saw him reading the Book of Revelation and asked whether he understood it.

"Yes, sir, I know what it means."

"You know what it means when Bible scholars have disagreed about it all these years! What do you think it means?"

"It means that Jesus is gonna win!"

Vance Havner said he doubted that a theologian could give a better summary of what the Book of Revelation means.[26]

Plan #3: Prepare a Specific Bible Lesson Thoroughly.

Of course, there must be diligent study of the specific Bible portion to be taught. There are no shortcuts. None that will make one a "workman who does not need to be ashamed and who correctly handles the word of truth."

If you speak only occasionally, pray for the Holy Spirit's guidance in choosing a passage to expound. If you faithfully read and meditate on His Word, you can claim Jesus' promise of the Spirit's guidance into all truth (John 16:13; cf. John 14:16, 17).

When you have prayerfully determined the Scripture passage, copy it on cards to carry in your pocket or purse or clip to the visor in your car. Refer to it frequently through the day. Ask the Lord to help you to grasp the author's meaning for those to whom it was written. Then, ask Him to help you apply it to your own life as you meditate on it.

The interpretation (meaning) must always precede the application (applying the truth to our lives). Reversing this order will make us liable to misinterpret Scripture. If we start out by asking, "What does this Scripture portion mean to me?" we might read into it meaning that is not actually in the passage, meaning the author did not intend. We must always make every effort to determine what the author meant. Claim James 1:5 in prayer—ask for wisdom.

Study the specific passage in context, the verses directly before and after your text.

Use evangelical, scholarly helps. Those available will vary according to the area of the world where you live. Probably the first and most readily available one is a good study Bible. The following paragraph is my personal testimony concerning the center-column references in many Bibles used to compare Scripture with Scripture:

I will never forget the thrill I had when I discovered that the little letters beside words in the Bible and corresponding letters in the center column indicated other verses on the same topic. I was eleven years old and had recently received the Lord Jesus Christ as my personal Savior. Although raised in a Christian home, I had never paid any attention to the letters and evidently no one had told me why they were there. Reading in Romans, I did not understand the word "justified" (3:24). The center-column references led me to several more verses and their center columns led to yet more. The Holy Spirit's teaching, using Scripture to interpret Scripture, took me on one of the greatest adventures of my life that afternoon—one that has never ceased after sixty-four years.

You do not develop a love for delicious, wholesome food by eating snack foods. And you cannot develop a love for the Word of God by reading or hearing what someone else says about it. The Bible is a feast set before us, Let's "come and dine" (cf. John. 21:12); as the song writer said, "You may feast at Jesus' table all the time."[27] As your study of the Bible grows, your love of it will become infectious and others will "catch it."

Perhaps one reason that "Through the Bible with J. Vernon McGee," has continued as the longest-running daily Christian radio broadcast in history—even continuing for years after his death—is that Dr. McGee's conversational and enthusiastic voice communicates his love for Bible study.

The *Treasury of Scripture Knowledge*[28] is a more thorough source of cross-references than the Bible's center-columns.

A good concordance is a basic tool for guidance in comparing Scriptures. You may have a short one in the back of your Bible. *Strong's*, *Young's*, and *Cruden's* Concordances, available from Christian bookstores, guide you to every word in the Bible every time it is used.

A commentary on the Bible book you are studying will help

you learn about the human author the Holy Spirit used to write it and the time, place, and people to whom it was written. It will give you facts that you may have missed in your study of the context. Bookstores can help you find the one you prefer.

Now, the Bible-study helps above and many others are available at our fingertips. Check the Logos Bible Software Web site at www.logosbiblesoftware.com. Whole libraries of helps are available on CDs for a fraction of the cost of the same materials in printed volumes.

Many Christian lay-workers for whom this book is written, may not have been able to study at a Bible college or seminary. Do not despair. William M. Easum, the 21st Century Church Strategist whom I quoted in my introduction, says, "Non-Christians seem to respond best to leaders who can communicate with them on their level more than leaders with academic credentials."[29]

Action International Ministries[30] has Project BookShare to help Christian workers in countries it serves. Christian Growth Ministries (Manila, The Philippines) has Project CLAIM (Christian Literature for Asians in Ministry). SIM International[31], provides Pastors' Book Sets in many countries. Overseas Missionary Fellowship publishes excellent books in the Orient. Operation Mobilization, New Life Literature, and other missions, publishers, and denominations have similar programs or libraries to help pastors, lay pastors, evangelists, teachers, and students. Ask your pastor or missionary what helps there are where you live. If you cannot afford them, ask whether there is a plan to help you.

Help For Christian Nationals, PO Box 381006, Duncanville, TX 75138, provides study and reference materials for pastors and Christian workers throughout Latin America and Asia. The primary tool supplied is *The Thompson Chain Reference Study Bible*. It contains a topical chain system with more than 4,200 topics, many in outline form. With two to three days of orientation any Christian worker can easily learn how to feed himself spiritually and prepare needed teaching which fits within his or her own cultural context. The *Thompson Bible* also includes a concordance, book studies, biographies, maps, historical background and many other practical ministry helps.

Sometimes the chapter and verses that will form your text will be obvious. It will simply be the next lesson or the next paragraph in the Bible portion your group is studying. If you are preaching a series of messages on a particular book of the Bible, you may start where you left off the previous week. However, you may prefer to select portions that highlight the overall teaching of some books. If you are giving a series on a Bible character, a chain-reference Bible, a study Bible or *Monser's Topical Index and Digest of the Bible* (Baker Book House, Grand Rapids, MI) will be a great help for finding all the references where the person's name is mentioned.

Your pastor or missionary may suggest others. But none will take the place of your faithful reading and prayerful meditation on the Word of God itself daily.

---

[1] Haddon W. Robinson, *Biblical Preaching* (Grand Rapids: Baker Book House, 1980), 10.

[2] Doreen Sears, "Doreen's Ukrainian Diary," Email Newsletter, Evangelical Free Church Mission, Nov. 1999.

[3] R. Arthur Mathews, *Born For Battle* (Robesonia, PA: OMF Books, 1978), 21.

[4] Harold Peters, "Live the Gospel," The Gospel Message 2000 Issue 1: 12.

[5] William M. Easum, "A Snapshot of the 21st Century Church," Strategies for Today's Leader Magazine.

[6] Dale Carnegie, *The Quick and Easy Way to Effective Speaking*; a revision by Dorothy Carnegie (New York: Pocket Books, 1962).

[7] Carnegie, 32

[8] John Newton, 1725-1807 (public domain)

[9] *The World Book Encyclopedia,* Vol. 8 (G); (Chicago: Field Enterprises, 1975), 341.

[10] Carnegie, 52.

[11] Bryan Chappell, *Christ-Centered Preaching* (Grand Rapids, Baker, 1994), 61, 62.

[12] Bryan Chappell, *Christ-Centered Preaching* , 319.

[13] "Olympic Games," *The World Book Encyclopedia*, 1975 ed.

[14] Bryan Chappell, *Christ-Centered Preaching*; 72.

[15] Sermon prepared and preached by Dr. Ted S. Rendall, Pastor Emeritus, The Prairie Tabernacle Congregation, Three Hills, Alberta, Canada, Feb. 27, 2000.

[16] Sermon Prepared and preached by Rev. Tom Peachey, Interim Pastor, Prairie Tabernacle Congregation, Three Hills, AB, Canada, Dec. 1999.

[17] *Sermons on Revival*, Charles H. Spurgeon, (Grand Rapids, Zondervan

Publishing House, 1958) publisher's jacket blurb.

[18] *Great Gospel Sermons*, Vol. II, Contemporary (London and Glasgow: Fleming H. Revell Co., 1949), 64.

[19] James Braga, *How to Prepare Bible Messages*, (Portland: Multnomah Press, 1981), 96.

[20] Jay E. Adams, *Pulpit Speech*, (Nutley, NJ: Presbyterian and Reformed Publishing Co., 1973) 54.

[21] Denis Lane, *Preach the Word* (Durham, England: Evangelical Press, 1986), 7, 8.

[22] Lane, 30, 31.

[23] Vance Havner, *Fourscore, Living Beyond the Promise*, (Old Tappan, New Jersey: Fleming H. Revell Co., 1982), 13.

[24] Anonymous

[25] "Come, Holy Spirit, Heavenly Dove," Isaac Watts, 1674-1748 (public domain)

[26] Vance Havner, *Fourscore, Living Beyond the Promise*, 55.

[27] C. B. Widmeyer, "Come and Dine," Copyright 1935, Renewal, J. T. Benson, owner

[28] *The Treasury of Scripture Knowledge*, Canne, Browne, Blayney, Scott & others (London, Bagster & Sons, and Westwood: Revell)

[29] Easum

[30] Action International Ministries (ACTION), PO Box 398 Mountlake Terrace, WA 98043-0398

[31] SIM Int., USA: PO Box 7900, Charlotte, NC 28241; CANADA: 10 Huntingdale Blvd., Scarborough, ON M1W 2Z5; UK: Wetheringsett Manor, Wetheringsett, Stowmarket, IP14 5QX

Other books available from...

Gabriel
Publishing

PO Box 1047
129 Mobilization Dr
Waynesboro, GA 30830

706-554-1594
1-8MORE-BOOKS
gabriel@omlit.om.org

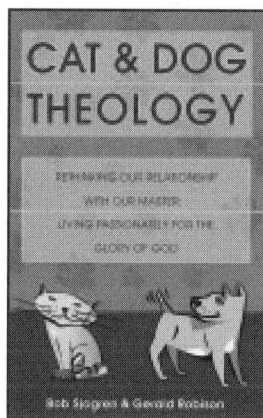

Cat and Dog Theology
Rethinking Our Relationship With Our Master

Bob Sjogren & Dr. Gerald Robison

There is a joke about cats and dogs that conveys their differences perfectly.

A dog says, "You pet me, you feed me, you shelter me, you love me, you must be God."
A cat says, "You pet me, you feed me, you shelter me, you love me, I must be God."

These God-given traits of cats ("You exist to serve me") and dogs ("I exist to serve you") are often similar to the theological attitudes we have in our view of God and our relationship to Him. Using the differences between cats and dogs in a light-handed manner, the authors compel us to challenge our thinking in deep and profound ways. As you are drawn toward God and the desire to reflect His glory in your life, you will worship, view missions, and pray in a whole new way. This life-changing book will give you a new perspective and vision for God as you delight in the God who delights in you.

1-884543-17-0   206 Pages

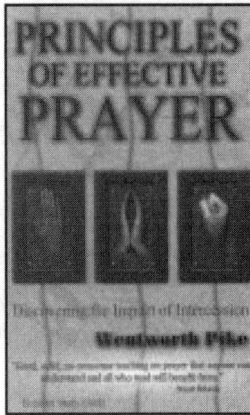

Principles Of Effective Prayer
Discovering The Impact Of Intercession

Wentworth Pike

What is prayer? Why pray? Created as a devotional study for individuals or a textbook for group, *Principles of Effective Prayer* answers these questions and many others. Developed as a class taught at Prairie Bible Institute (Canada), this book will lead you into a life and ministry of effective, God-glorifying prayer! Thousands of students have discovered dynamic prayer through Pike's teaching – now you can too.

"Good, solid, no-nonsense teaching on prayer that anyone can understand and all who read will benefit from."

Stuart Briscoe
Minister-at-Large, Elmbrook Church

1-884543-65-0   290 Pages

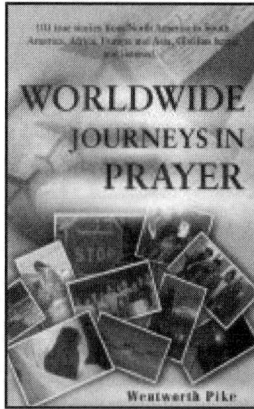

Worldwide Journeys In Prayer
101 True Stories Of Prayer From Around The World

Wentworth Pike

Ranging in topics from suffering, guidance and protection to soul-winning prayer, Wentworth Pike has allowed us a glimpse into the lives of those who are serving God and seeking His face worldwide.

> "These stories of answered prayers and lessons the Lord teaches us through prayer...will challenge each of us to depend on God in new ways and cause our business-as-usual prayers to be one of expectancy and anticipation."
>
> Jim Raymo
> U.S. Director of WEC International

1-884543-66-9   418 Pages

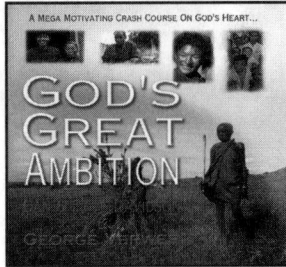

God's Great Ambition
A Mega-Motivating Crash Course On God's Heart

Dan and Dave Davidson
and George Verwer

This unique collection of quotes and Scriptures has been designed to motivate thousands of people into action in world missions. George Verwer and the Davidsons are well-known for their ministries of mission mobilization as speakers and writers.

Turn to any page and get ready to be encouraged and respond with an increase of awareness, action and ownership in sharing God's good news around His world.

1-884543-69-3   208 Pages

Operation World
Patrick Johnstone & Jason Mandryk

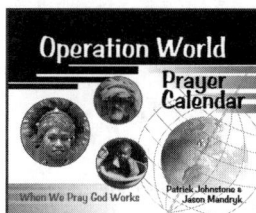

Prayer Calendar

This spiral desk calendar contains clear graphics and useful geographic, cultural, economic, and political statistics on 122 countries of the world. The *Operation World Prayer Calendar* is a great tool to help you pray intelligently for the world. Pray for each country for three days and see how God works!

1-884543-59-6   256 Pages

Wall Map
22" x 36"

This beautiful, full-color wall map is a great way to locate the countries that you are praying for each day and build a global picture. Not only an excellent resource for schools, churches, and offices, but a valuable tool for the home.

1-884543-60-X	Laminated
1-884543-61-8	Folded

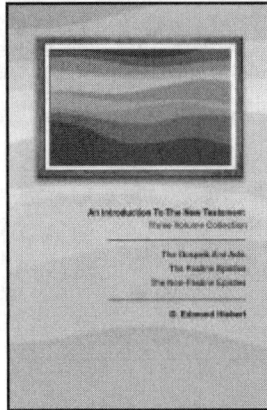

An Introduction To The New Testament
Three Volume Collection

D. Edmond Hiebert

Though not a commentary, the Introduction to the New Testament presents each book's message along with a discussion of such questions as authorship, composition, historical circumstances of their writing, issues of criticism and provides helpful, general information on their content and nature. The bibliographies and annotated book list will be extremely helpful for pastors, teachers and laymen as an excellent invitation to further careful exploration.

This book will be prized by all that have a desire to delve deeply into the New Testament writings.

> Volume 1: The Gospels And Acts
> Volume 2: The Pauline Epistles
> Volume 3: The Non-Pauline Epistles and Revelation

1-884543-74-X   976 Pages